The Stock Market Show

The First Step Towards Your Trading Journey

SAHIL A BAGDIYA

I would like to dedicate this book to my parents & my brother who always supported in every situation & encouraged me to improve everyday.

I am also greatful to those who pushed me to aim higher & keep working hard!!

Contents

Disclaimer

The risk involved in trading is considerable which should not be ignored. Trade at your own risk as per your comfort. Neither the author, nor the publisher would be responsible for any losses incurred for acting on any trading setup explained in this book.

This book is purely for educational purpose only.

Introduction

This book is my attempt to bring all the information about the stock market in one place in as simple language as possible so that even a common man/woman can understand it with utmost ease. In this book we will be looking at the various concepts of the Stock Market.

Consider this book as a small package of various concepts of stock market, from the basics to the complexities of intraday and options trading along with the importance of analysis and the major role played by psychology in trading. At the end of this book, I will also clear the doubts and myths related to stock market.

In this book you will get almost everything you might need to start your journey in a stock market (Except for the Capital).

I won't be discussing about the history, establishment and other things that according to me won't help you in the stock market. But if you want to know about these things you can search the web as per your convenience.

I will try my level best to explain the concepts in layman's terms. I will guide you slowly and step by step through various topics with the help of charts and examples wherever needed, so that you don't get lost in between.

What I want is for you to complete reading this book before entering the markets and not do the opposite. But if you have already entered the market and things didn't go as you have planned then don't worry it is never too late for anything. I know that this book will help you to get going further and bounce back even stronger.

I will also advise you not to enter the markets immediately after you are done reading this book. This book will definitely clear your concepts but that doesn't mean you should start trading immediately. There is a lot to learn. You should only enter after you have done your own research and have gained enough knowledge about the benefits and drawbacks involved in trading in stock market.

I won't take much time as we have so much to cover ahead of us. So, without wasting more time let's get started.

1. BASICS OF THE STOCK MARKET

Stock market is just like a market where you buy and sell different kinds of goods. Imagine it as buying/selling fruits in a supermarket. But in the stock market instead of fruits you are buying/selling shares of companies listed on the stock exchange. The only difference between a supermarket and a stock market is that the goods/products in a supermarket are usually bought/sold by visiting the stores physically while stock market trading is done in electronic form. Stock market can be accessed electronically from your mobile/computer and trading is done in a dematerialized form.

In India there are two main stock exchanges, **Bombay Stock Exchange** (BSE) and **National Stock Exchange** (NSE). There are about **5,000** listed companies on the BSE, while NSE has more than **1,600** companies listed on its platform. The India Stock Market is regulated by **Securities and Exchange Board of India** (SEBI). The market is regulated for obvious reasons such as fair-trading practices and to avoid frauds or scams.

Sensex and Nifty are broad market indices and benchmarks of equity market. Sensex comprises of top 30 companies listed on BSE, whereas Nifty comprises of top 50 companies listed on NSE. The index reflects the general market trend for the selected period. While Sensex and Nifty represent the broader markets, certain indices represent specific sectors known as the sectoral indices. For example, Bank Nifty index on NSE represents the performance specific to the banking industry. Both BSE and NSE have sector-specific indexes.

You need a **Demat** and a Bank account to start your trading journey. So, what exactly is a DEMAT account?

When someone buy shares, those shares are credited into their Depository account, usually referred to as the DEMAT account. It is maintained electronically by two companies in India, The Central Depository Services Limited (**CDSL**) and National Securities Depository Limited (**NSDL**). These depositories act as a vault for the shares that you buy and hold your shares. You can consider Depository as your bank account. Your money is kept in bank account whereas your shares are kept in a Demat account maintained by the depositories. A bank account has to be linked to the Demat account for adding funds into your trading account.

Domestic Retail Participants (Retailers) are people like us transacting in markets, whereas those people who are of Indian origin but based outside India are NRI's and OCI. Large corporate entities based in India are called Domestic Institutions example LIC.

When we buy or sell shares from stock exchange it is done through a registered stockbroker. **Stock Brokers** are the trading members of the stock exchange who provides services to the end client like us. In India, there are many stockbrokers like AngelOne, Upstox, Zerodha, etc. Once we place our buy/sell order on the trading platform the stockbroker finds the seller/buyer and then our order gets executed. All this happens within few seconds. You can either place a limit order or a market order for buying or selling shares. In Limit order the trade gets executed at the price entered by us, if there is no seller for the price we have entered, the order won't be executed, whereas in Market Order the trade will be executed at the price prevailing in the markets at the time of placing the order.

There are some commonly used Jargons you might have heard on news channels or from someone you know such as bullish/bearish market, all time high, etc.

Bullish market (Tezi) means that the market is moving in an upward direction i.e., market is in uptrend, whereas **Bearish market (Mandi)** means that the market is moving in a downward direction i.e., market is in downtrend. Needless to explain, Bulls are those who push the market upwards and Bears are those who pull the market down.

52 week high/ 52 week low refers to the high or low made by a particular stock during the time period of 52 weeks i.e., 1 year, whereas all time high or low refers to the lifetime high or low made by the stock from the time it was listed on the exchange.

A company deciding to go public, essentially means that the company is offering its shares to the public in exchange for funds known as **Initial Public Offer (IPO)**. A company may decide to file for an IPO for various reasons such as raising funds, repaying of debts, etc. An IPO is said to be oversubscribed when the bids received are more than the shares issue whereas, it is said to be undersubscribed when bids received are less than shares issue. For example, if a company issues 10,000 shares to the public and receives bids for 15,000 shares, it is said to be the situation of oversubscription, whereas if a company receives bids for only 8,000 shares out of 10,000 shares issued then it is the situation of undersubscription.

There is a concept of **Grey Market Premium** (GMP) that pops out when the IPO's hit the market and the company is about to list on the stock exchange.

So, what really is GMP? To understand that you must know what IPO grey market is.

It is unofficial market where company's shares are bid unofficially. This takes place before the shares are even issued by the company in an IPO. There are no rules and regulations. Regulators like SEBI are not involved in these transactions. They don't endorse this either. Grey Markets are generally run by a small set of individuals. All deals are based on mutual trust.

Grey Market Premium is nothing but the price at which the shares are being traded in grey market. To conclude for investors like us, the GMP can be seen as an indicator of how the stock might perform after it gets listed, and when the company lists at the price higher than its issue price it is said to be listed at premium. If the company gets listed at price lower than its issue price it is said to be listed at discount.

Now I hope that whenever you hear someone talk about Grey Markets and GMP you won't feel left out and you might even give them a thought or two.

Moving further we will talk about Dividend, Bonus Issue, Right Issue, Buyback of shares and Stock Split one by one.

To start with **Dividends**, they are cash pay-outs made to distribute profits made by the company during year. Dividends are paid on per share basis. You can consider it as interest you receive on your money in your bank account or on Fixed Deposits. For example, if you have 1,000 Shares of ITC and the company declares a dividend of Rs 5/share then you are entitled to receive Rs 5,000 as dividend which will be credited directly into your bank account linked with your demat account. The company may or may not declare dividend every year.

There are some terms related to dividend that you should know. The date on which company's board approves the dividend in the Annual General Meeting (AGM) is called the **Dividend Declaration Date**. The date on which company reviews the shareholders register to list down all the eligible shareholders for the dividend is known as the **Record Date**. An investor must be listed on that date to be eligible for a dividend pay-out. Then there is **Ex-Date** or **Ex-Dividend Date,** the ex-date is usually one or two business day before the date of record. You will be eligible for the dividend "only" if you buy the shares before the ex-dividend date.

At last, the date on which the dividends are paid out to shareholders and the money is directly credited to the bank account linked with DEMAT account as stated earlier is known as **Dividend Payout Date**. There's one more thing you should know, the price of the stock gets reduced by the dividend amount on ex-dividend date. For example, if company with a share price of Rs 100 declares a dividend of Rs 5 per share then its price will be reduced to Rs 95 per share on ex-dividend date.

Now moving onto **Bonus Issue**, think of it as dividend, but here you get free shares against shares that you hold. There is bonus announcement date, ex-bonus date and record date similar to the dividend issue. Bonus shares are allotted in the fixed ratio such as 1:1, 2:1 etc. For example, if the ratio is 2:1, the existing shareholders will get 2 additional shares for every 1 share held by them without any additional cost. So, if you own 500 shares, then you will receive an additional 1,000 shares increasing the total number of shares to 1,500.

In case of bonus issue, only the number of shares held by shareholders increases but the overall value of investment remains same.

To explain this, look at the table 1.1 on the next page:

Bonus Issue	Shares before Bonus	Share Price before Bonus	Total Investment before	Share Price after Bonus	Total Shares after Bonus	Total Investment after
1:1	100	120	12,000	60	200	12,000
3:2	40	625	25,000	250	100	25,000
5:3	3000	15	45,000	5.625	8000	45,000

Table 1.1

Bonus shares are issued to encourage participation of retailers like you and me, especially when price per share of company is very high and is difficult for new investors to buy shares. In case of bonus issue the face value remains unchanged, only the number of outstanding shares increases. The shares are credited after a few days (usually 15 days after the ex-date).

The "**Stock Split**" is another regularly occurring corporate action (Shown in Table 1.2). In simple terms it means splitting a stock. Yes, it is that simple! When stock split is declared by the company, the number of shares increases, the investment value remains the same just like the bonus issue. The only difference between bonus issue and stock split is that in stock split the face value changes whereas in bonus issue it doesn't. In stock splits the shares with a new face value are credited immediately. Suppose the face value of the stock is Rs 10, and there is a 1:2 stock split, then the face value will change to Rs 5. If you owned 100 shares before the split, you would now own 200 shares after the split (Old Face value being 10).

Split Ratio	Shares held before split	Share Price before split	New FV	Shares held after split	Share Price after split	Investment before and after split
1:2	100	1200	5	200	600	1,20,000
1:4	25	750	2.5	100	187.5	18,750

Table 1.2

Reverse Stock Split is opposite of stock split. It is a measure taken by companies to reduce their number of outstanding shares in the market. Existing shares are consolidated into fewer, proportionally more valuable, shares, resulting in a boost to the company's stock price. For example, in a one-for-ten (1:10) reverse split, shareholders receive one share of the company's new stock for every 10 shares that they owned. In other words, a shareholder who held 1,000 shares would end up with 100 shares after the reverse stock split was complete. The total value of the shares an investor holds also remains unchanged.

Right issue is done to raise fresh capital. But here instead of going public, the company approaches their existing shareholders. It's just like a 2nd IPO but for a selected group of people (Existing shareholders). The shareholders can subscribe to the rights issue in the proportion of their shareholding. For example, imagine a company trading at Rs 200 per share offers a 1:4 rights issue. It means for every 4 shares a shareholder owns he can subscribe to 1 additional share. The new shares under the rights issue will be issued at a lower price than the price prevailing in the markets. So, the new shares can be subscribed to at say, Rs 165 per share, a discount of 17.5%.

However, one should not buy the shares only because they are available at discount. Here you are paying money to acquire shares unlike bonus issue. Therefore, you should only subscribe if you are convinced and confident about the future of the company. Next on our list is Buyback.

Buyback is when the company invests in itself by buying shares from other investors in the market. It reduces the number of shares outstanding in the market. There could be many reasons why company choose to buy back shares such as improving the profitability on a per-share basis, to prevent other companies from taking over, to support the share price from declining in the markets, etc. In short, when a company announces a buyback, it shows that the company is confident about its future and is positive for the price of share.

At last, as you might have already known, there is a seller for every buyer and buyer for every seller in the stock market. People buy shares in order to earn short term or long-term capital gains and dividend-based income. There is a concept of Short Selling also known as "Shorting" or "going short". In short selling, traders can sell first at a higher price and then buy at a lower price. You might be thinking, how can we sell something that we don't have?

Short selling is done to gain when the price of an underlying is falling. It is done by borrowing the shares the trader wishes to short sell from market, then selling at high and buying back at low prices. The difference between the sell price and the buy price is the short seller's profit.

The shares are returned to the lender when the short seller buys them back. Short selling should be done only by experienced investors and traders as the losses can be huge and unimaginable. For example, consider a trader has shorted a stock at the price of Rs.250 per share. The price of the stock can keep on increasing forever. Whereas, if a trader buys 100 shares at Rs.250 each, the maximum loss can only be the amount invested, i.e., Rs.25,000. These are the situations where the stop loss plays an important role as it stops the loss at a particular level indicating you to exit the position. Hence, only experienced investors who have high risk tolerance and understands the risk associated with short selling should try it. An alternate option for short selling is to buy a put option of the same stock. Options will be discussed later in this book.

That will be all for this chapter. I hope this chapter has cleared your basic concepts related to the stock market.

Let us now move onto our next chapter where we will discuss why we should invest.

2. WHY SHOULD ONE INVEST?

"How many millionaires do you know who have become wealthy by investing in savings accounts? I rest my case."

- *Robert G. Allen*

Investing your hard-earned money in assets which can generate enough returns to sustain through your retired life is very important. Investing is a lifelong affair and one should have an efficient plan to save and invest throughout the working years.

But what will investing benefit us? What if we choose not to invest? Let us figure that out.

Let's say you earn 50K per month, out of that, you spend 35K towards your daily expenses, now you will have 15K surplus in your hand every month. You decide not to invest the monthly surplus amount and leave it as it is.

At this rate how much money will you be left with by the time you retire? Suppose you are 25 years old now and plan to retire at the age of 50 meaning that you have 25 years of working left. You don't want to work after your retirement. Assuming your expenses will be fixed. The balance of 15K per month is kept in your savings bank account. All other factors being constant you earn Rs 6,00,000 per year out of which you save Rs 1,80,000 every year.

Have a look at the table 2.1 below: -

Years	Income per year	Expense per year	Savings per year
1 to 25	6,00,000	4,20,000	1,80,000
		Total Savings after retirement	**45,00,000**

Table 2.1

So, at this rate when you retire (after 25 years) you will have total savings of 45 lakhs. As your expenses remain same i.e., 4,20,000 per year you can take care of your expenses roughly for 11 Years. But what after that? What will you do after you run out of all of your savings? Not to forget, we have avoided the inflation which will increase your expenses every year, taxes you have to pay, unexpected situations which might increase expense such as medical expenses. You will surely get a hike in your salary yearly but I don't think that it will be enough for you to take care of your expenses after you don't have any savings left.

Now consider this, instead of keeping the cash idle, you choose to invest it in an investment option which grows at 10% per annum (yearly). For example, at the end of the 1st year you saved Rs 1,80,000 and decided to invest this amount for next 24 years (Growing 10% yearly). The 2nd year you did the same thing and invested your savings for the next 23 years, this kept going till the time when you retire.

Have a look at the table 2.2 on the next page to get a much better view about the scenario.

Years	Income	Expense	Savings	Investment value at the time of retirement*
1	6,00,000	4,20,000	1,80,000	17,72,952
2	6,00,000	4,20,000	1,80,000	16,11,774
3	6,00,000	4,20,000	1,80,000	14,65,250
4	6,00,000	4,20,000	1,80,000	13,32,045
5	6,00,000	4,20,000	1,80,000	12,10,950
6	6,00,000	4,20,000	1,80,000	11,00,864
7	6,00,000	4,20,000	1,80,000	10,00,785
8	6,00,000	4,20,000	1,80,000	9,09,804
9	6,00,000	4,20,000	1,80,000	8,27,095
10	6,00,000	4,20,000	1,80,000	7,51,905
11	6,00,000	4,20,000	1,80,000	6,83,550
12	6,00,000	4,20,000	1,80,000	6,21,409
13	6,00,000	4,20,000	1,80,000	5,64,917
14	6,00,000	4,20,000	1,80,000	5,13,561
15	6,00,000	4,20,000	1,80,000	4,66,874
16	6,00,000	4,20,000	1,80,000	4,24,430
17	6,00,000	4,20,000	1,80,000	3,85,845

18	6,00,000	4,20,000	1,80,000	3,50,770
19	6,00,000	4,20,000	1,80,000	3,18,880
20	6,00,000	4,20,000	1,80,000	2,89,892
21	6,00,000	4,20,000	1,80,000	2,63,538
22	6,00,000	4,20,000	1,80,000	2,39,580
23	6,00,000	4,20,000	1,80,000	2,17,800
24	6,00,000	4,20,000	1,80,000	1,98,000
25	6,00,000	4,20,000	1,80,000	1,80,000
			Total Saving after Retirement	**1,77,02,470**

Table 2.2

*Rounding off to nearest number

At the end of 24 years, the investment made in 1st year will grow to Rs. 17,72,952 and the 2nd years investment will grow to Rs. 16,11,774.

If you add up all the final values, you will get a total of more than 1.7 Crores, which is more than 3.5 times higher than what you would have saved without investing.

This according to me will clear the air around the question of why we need to invest. It also might have convinced you to invest. But the next important question that you might have in mind is – Where should we invest?

Before investing you should choose an appropriate asset which matches your risk profile (risk you can take). Risk taking capacity can differ from person to person.

Some of the most popular assets one can invest in are:

- Real Estates

- Equity

- Gold

- Fixed income instruments such as Fixed Deposits, Bonds, etc.

One should make sure that they invest wisely so that they get good returns on the investments made for risk undertaken, maintaining a good risk to reward ratio. Risk to Reward ratio is one of the most important things that should be taken care of while investing/trading. Higher the risk, higher is the return and vice versa.

Investment in **Real Estate** involves buying and selling of commercial and non-commercial land. Here you can generate returns by way of rental income and the capital appreciation of property. The process of buying and selling involves legal verification of documents, the amount of cash required is also usually large. So, it can be quite complex.

Investment in **Equities** (Shares) means buying shares of listed companies available on exchanges such as BSE and NSE. The returns from equity investment can be extremely attractive. But there is also risk involved. Indian equities have generated returns close to 15% CAGR (Compound Annual Growth Rate) over past 10 Years. One more thing that might attract you to invest in equities is that the profits generated over long term period (more than 12 months) attracts just 10% tax, with first 1 lakh being exempted from tax.

One of the safest investments considered is the investments made in **Gold & Silver**. Over a long-term period, gold and silver have appreciated in value. Investments in these metals have resulted in returns of approximately 7-8% over the last 20 Years.

Fixed income instruments are assets with limited downside risk and limited return. Returns in these instruments are in form of interest payment. Generally, the return from fixed income instrument varies between 7% and 10%. If you want to protect your capital and earn a moderate return then investments in fixed deposit is the way to go for you.

Investments should be allocated in a mix of all asset classes. As the famous saying goes "Never put all your eggs in one basket". Investment varies according to risk taking capacity of an individual. Those who are young can take high risk and invest accordingly whereas, a retired person could invest his savings in more safe assets.

This might have answered your questions about why and where to invest. I encourage you to start investing as early as possible. You can even start with amount as small as 500. But remember Rs. 500 Monthly for 5 years amounts to the investment of Rs. 30K. But invest after doing your own research not just because someone you know have told you to do so.

By now, you might have understood that investing can do great wonders, if done right. The only key to investing is doing proper analysis and investing in fundamentally strong companies with great future. If you have invested in the right company then it will most probably reward you with good returns over the long run resulting into a wealth creator, but if the company you have invested in is not good then it can also prove to be a wealth destroyer (we will see this while discussing about fundamental analysis).

17

Having said that, now you might have a good reason to start investing.

In the next chapter we will see how and why the price of stocks move.

3. WHAT MAKES THE PRICE OF A STOCK MOVE?

You are the one who is moving the price of a stock!!

Yes, the people like us are moving the price of a stock. The price is driven by the demand in the market for a particular stock. But there are many other factors that makes a stock move up or down. Prices also move if there is any news related to the company which is listed on the stock exchange. We will discuss various such factors that might change the price of a stock in this chapter.

Consider this, Infosys releases its annual results on April 13 at 4 p.m. and reports an increase in its net profit by 5,500 Crores 12% more than the previous year. According to you, what will be the effect of this news on the stock of Infosys? It will move up obviously as this is a positive news for the company.

When positive announcements are made by companies, the market participants tend to buy the stock at any given price, which ultimately results into the rally of the stock price.

We will try to understand the effect of this news on the price of stock when markets open in next trading session with the help of table 3.1 on the next page.

Time	Current Market Price (CMP)	Seller's Price	Buyer's action	New Last Traded Price (LTP)
10:03	1735	1737	Buys	1737
10:04	1737	1739	Buys	1739
10:06	1739	1742	Buys	1742
10:08	1742	1751	Buys	1751

Table 3.1

What did you notice here?

You can see that buyers are ready to buy the stock at whatever price the seller wants. As a result, the stock price gave an upside move of 16 Rupees in 5 minutes. Even though this is a fictional situation, it is quite realistic. You can see stock price move greatly in just few minutes.

Moving ahead, consider a company reported loss in its results and is about to close some of its businesses. As this was a negative news and will have a great impact on the stock, what do you think would've happened? How would the price react to such news?

You've guessed it right; people will start booking profits/sell the stock which will ultimately lead the price of the stock to fall. (One might also choose to hold the stock for long term and find a buying opportunity as per their risk appetite).

Look at the table 3.2 below to understand:

Time	Current Market Price (CMP)	Seller's Price	Buyer's action	New Last Traded Price (LTP)
11:43	2125	2123	Sells	2123
11:45	2123	2120	Sells	2120
11:46	2120	2115	Sells	2115
11:49	2115	2113	Sells	2113

Table 3.2

This shows that the market participants react to news and their reaction results into price movements! This is what would usually happen in the circumstances when there is a positive or negative news in a stock. But what happens when there is no news in a stock? Do you think that the price will stay flat and not move at all?

Well, this depends on the company in focus. Suppose there are two companies Company X Ltd and Company Y Ltd. X Ltd is one of the largest companies in the country with great fundamentals and Y Ltd is less known as compared to X Ltd.

If you were to buy the shares of one company from these two, which company's share would you prefer to buy? Definitely X Ltd. Reason is simple, as X Ltd is one of the largest company market participants would like to buy or sell the shares, whether there is news or not, this results in a constant movement of the price.

In other case, as Y Ltd is less known and might not attract the market participant's attention. Under such circumstances the price of such company may not move or the move may be very small.

Price may also move due to other events such as news related to particular industry or economy as a whole. Events such as war, political tensions, increasing inflation, etc. For example, during the recent event of war between Russia and Ukraine the worldwide market was falling as you might have observed or heard on the news.

Some other events that might change the prices of stocks in market (price will change only if the news has an effect on the stock or related to the industry), are Monetary policy, Change in RBI rates (Repo Rate and Reverse Repo Rate), Change in CRR, Budget announcement, etc.

To summarize, stock prices can be driven by news and events but, even if there is no news, the price moves owing to the demand and supply for the stock in the market.

This was the short and simple explanation of how the price of various stocks moves.

Next, we will look at effect on the price of stocks under various circumstances with the help of charts for understanding this more clearly. We will use Black and White candles instead of red and green candles respectively while understanding the chart patterns and candlestick signals.

Effect of dividend in BPCL on its price:

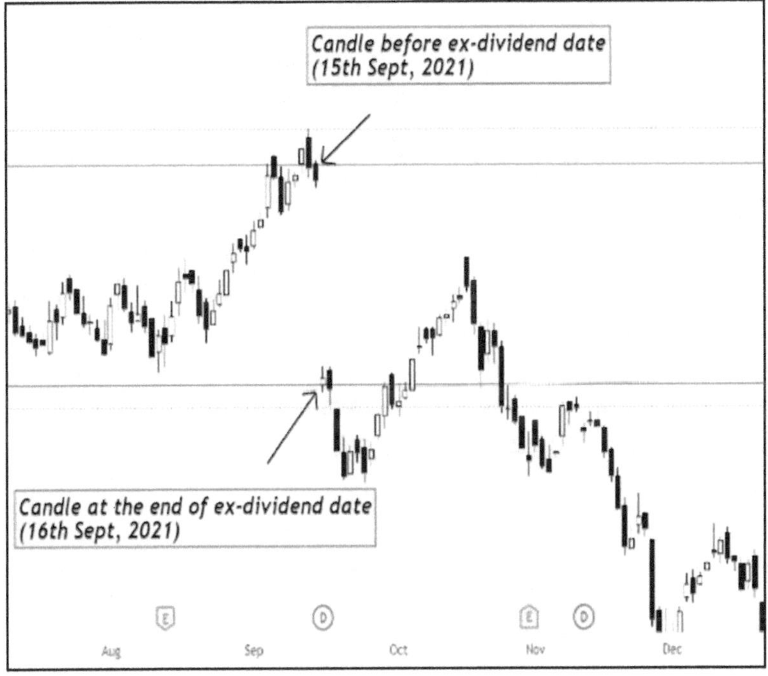

Chart 3.1

BPCL announced to give special dividend of Rs.58 per share and set 16th September 2021 as ex-date. So, in order to be eligible for the dividend you must buy share before ex-date i.e., till 15th September 2021. You can see chart 3.1 above that the price of BPCL got reduced from almost 494 to 436 which is same as the dividend amount per share i.e., Rs.58

Effect of negative news in Infosys on its price:

Chart 3.2

There was negative news related to Infosys after markets closed on 18th October,2019 (Saturday). There was a trading holiday on Monday i.e., 21st October, 2019. You can see from chart 3.2 above that as markets opened on 22nd October, 2019, Infosys opened with huge gap-down. It almost fell from Rs.765 to Rs.643 per share i.e., by Rs.124 at the day end which is close to 16%

Effect of positive news in on its price:

Chart 3.3

IT company Wipro posted a 17 per cent jump in consolidated net profit to Rs 2,930.6 crore for the quarter ended on September 30, 2021, on 13th October,2021 which resulted into big gap-up and upside move in stock price from Rs.672 to Rs.706 i.e., more than 5%

You can see that later in the chart 3.3, there was a huge fall again in the price of stock. I want you to find out what lead that fall in the price.

General Price movement:

Chart 3.4

Above, in chart 3.4, we can see Reliance Industries on daily timeframe where we can see that generally the price of a stock moves up and down due to demand and supply. This is what generally happens in stocks, when the demand is high the price moves more and when the demand is less then price will move slightly.

Want to see what happened in the markets when everyone was forced to be at their home due to lockdown in 2020 because of Corona Virus or even when Russia attacked Ukraine in 2022?

Let us have a look at what happened in 2020:

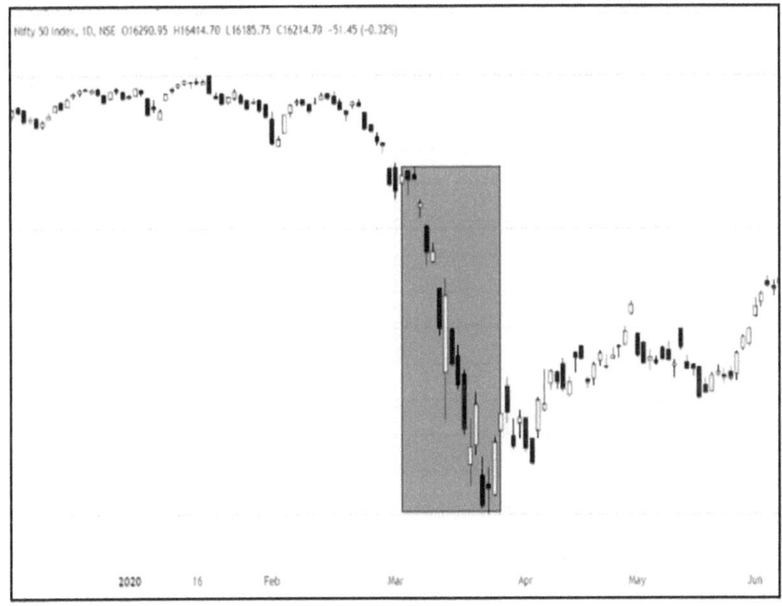

Chart 3.5

Focus on the marked area in chart 3.5 (from 4th March, 2020 to 25th March 2020), here you can see that the news of COVID-19 was very bad news for the markets which lead the Nifty Index to fall from **11,267.80** to **7511.10** within of 20 days which was more than **32%**.

Talking about what happened at the time when Russia attacked Ukraine recently, I will leave it up to you. I know you can easily find that out on your own now.

This will be all about the movements of stock prices. I hope you understood how it works. Do look and study some of the companies' performances during various situations and their price movements to get a better grasp.

The next topic on our list is the Fundamental and Technical analysis which will be discussed in the next chapter.

4. WHAT IS MEANT BY FUNDAMENTAL AND TECHNICAL ANALYSIS?

Fundamental Analysis (FA):

Fundamental Analysis (FA) refers to studying the business as a whole. When an investor looks to invest in a business for the long term i.e., 2-5 years or even more, it becomes an extremely essential task to understand the business from various angles. If a company is fundamentally strong, then it will be reflected in its share price sooner or later in the long run, resulting into wealth creation for its investors. This is a vast concept which requires a detailed study about the topic. I will try to summarize this topic so that you can get an idea about what Fundamental Analysis is.

You may have heard many times that if you have invested 1 lakh in share of a particular company 10 to 20 years ago it would have grown to be 10 times now. We have many such examples in the Indian market, like TCS, Sun Pharma, Reliance Industries, etc. which have generated multifold returns for its investors over the long term. Let us have a look at some of them with the help of charts.

On the next page we have the Chart of **TCS** (Chart 4.1) showing consistence growth. It has grown from Rs.517 per share in 2012 to almost Rs.3700 per share in 2022 which is more than 7 times.

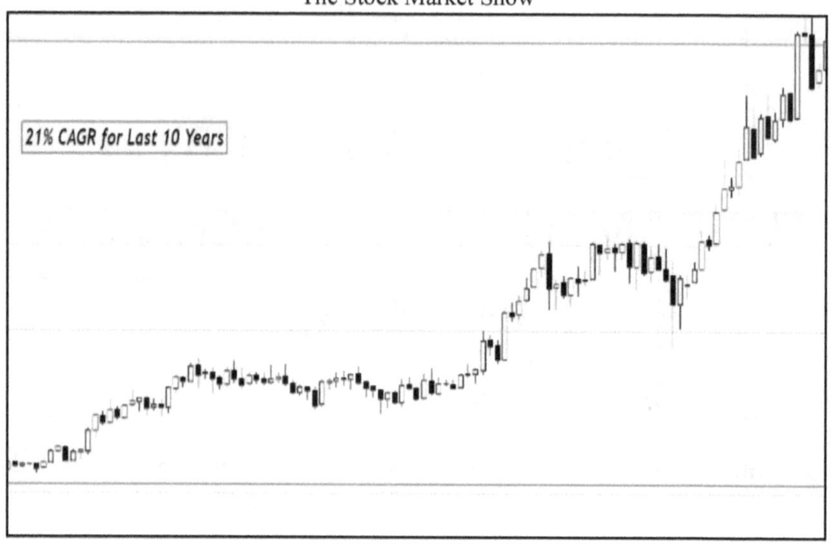

Chart 4.1

Next, we have **Reliance Industries** (chart 4.2), this too has shown an incredible growth. It grew from Rs.344/share in 2012 to more than Rs.2,500/share in 2022. This stock too has grown 7 times giving 21% CAGR for past 10 years.

Chart 4.2

In chart 4.3, you can see that **Sun Pharma** grew from Rs.250 per share in 2012 to more than Rs.900 per share in 2022 which is close to 4 times (12% CAGR for last 10 years).

Chart 4.3

(It did fall from its high of 1,200/share to the levels of almost 300/share in 2020 but it recovered from that and have grown 3 times in 2 years. That is what generally happens with companies with strong fundamentals, even after falling they can bounce back)

BUT!! There are always two sides of a coin, if you have invested in fundamentally weak stocks or those having heavy debt and various other issues then it could turn to be a disaster for you and can cause unparalleled damage. There are some examples of such companies which turned out to be wealth destroyers which we will see with the help of charts.

Reliance Capital:

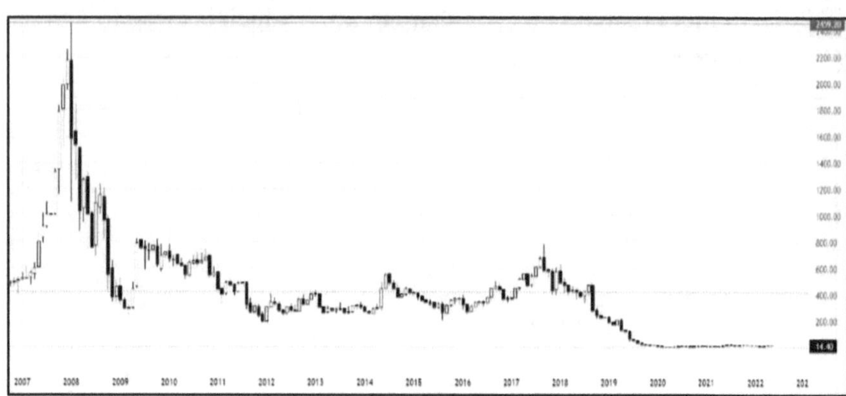

Chart 4.4

From the chart above (4.4) we can clearly see that the price fell from Rs.2,400/share in 2008 to Rs.14/share in 2022 creating negative returns for the investors.

JP Power:

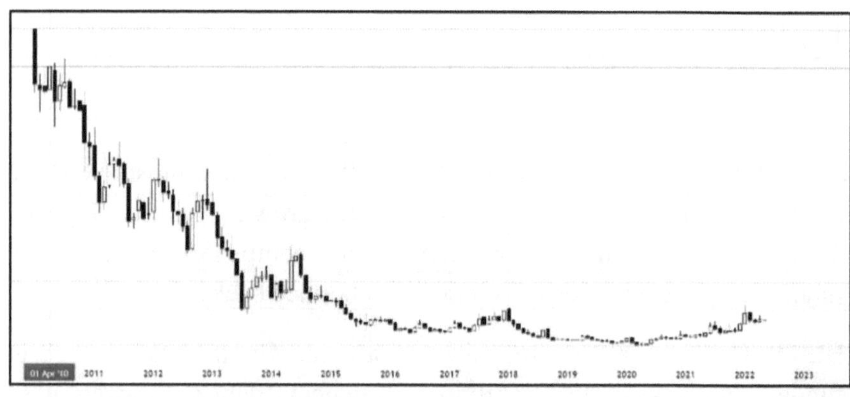

Chart 4.5

This stock also fell from Rs.74/share in 2011 to less than Rs.8/share in 2022 which is close to 90%. This means if you would have invested 1 lakh in JP Power on 1st April, 2010, then you would be left with only Rs.10,000.

Vodafone Idea Ltd:

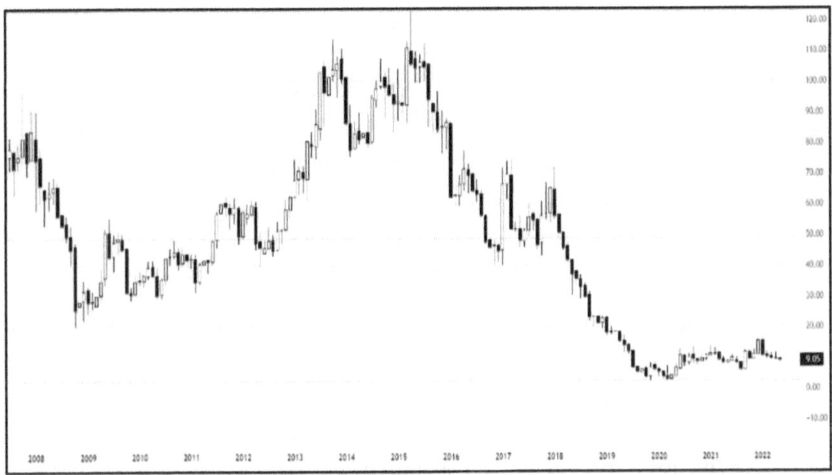

Chart 4.6

This stock was above Rs.50/share in 2012 making an all-time high of 123 in April,2015. You can see that it is trading at Rs.9.05/share at the time of writing this book (23rd May, 2022).

These are just few examples of stocks which turned into wealth creators and wealth destroyers amongst the many you may find in the Indian Markets. You can find a right company to invest in with the help of "Fundamental Analysis".

But the question here is, how to do fundamental analysis? Can only those who are from commerce background or those having a professional degree be good fundamental analysts?

The straightforward answer is, **NO**!

You just need few basic skills to understand the fundamentals of a company such as basic mathematical operations (addition, subtraction, division and multiplication), understanding the basic financial statements such as Profit and loss statement, Balance sheet, Cashflow

Statement, etc. and understanding the business in which the company operates. Once you find a company with strong fundamentals and which won't get affected by the ups and downs of the market in the long run, you can invest in it with conviction.

There are few characteristics of the companies, in which you can consider about investing, which can be classified under Qualitative and Quantitative aspects. To find a fundamentally strong company one should study both the aspects.

The Qualitative aspect mainly involves understanding:

- Management's background whether they are able to run the business or not, their qualifications and check whether there are any criminal cases against the promoters if any.

- Appointment of directors, organization structure, transparency, etc.

- Is the management involved in scams, bribery, unfair business practices?

- Is management paying themselves a large sum of salary, usually a percentage of profits?

- Is their operator activity involved in the stock?

- Does the business require political support constantly?

If any of the factors mentioned above does not fall in right place & you plan to invest in such company then you are definitely playing with fire and might burn your hands!

The Quantitative aspects are matters related to financial data which mainly includes things such as:

- Profitability and its growth

- Earnings

- Cashflows from various activities

- Dividend payouts

- Taxes paid

- Asset growth

- Investments

- Financial ratios, etc.

Now you might be thinking that doing fundamental analysis and studying the qualitative and quantitative aspects may involve complicated process. But this is where it gets interesting.

It can be done using extremely basic tools/documents such as Annual report of the company, data related to the industry, daily news. This is all that you might need for fundamental analysis and you are good to go. The main objective is to keep the research simple and logical.

So, what is an Annual Report and what does it contain?

Annual reports are documents designed to provide readers with information about a company's performance in previous year which is published by the end of a financial year. It is usually available on the company's website. They contain information such as Performance/Financial highlights, a letter from the CEO, financial information (such as Income Statement, Balance Sheet and Statement of Cashflows) and objectives and goals for future years. It contains the auditor's certificates (signed, dated, and sealed) certifying the reliability of the financial data included in the annual report. To understand more about Annual reports let us discuss its content.

Performance/Financial Highlights:

This section usually highlights some of the company's key achievements, goals reached or awards received by the company or its employees. It generally consists of multi-year comparison of the growth in revenue, sales, profits, etc. In this section company can also include few financial ratios (more on ratios later), which are calculated by the company itself. You can consider this section as a bird's eye view of the company's previous year.

A letter from CEO:

CEOs typically spends a lot of time on their letters to highlight the company's achievements, as its performance is relative to the industry it operates in. It gives us a sense of what the management of the company has to say about their business.

Objectives and goals for future years provide shareholders with information on the company's future goals and objectives. This helps the potential investors to get a thorough understanding of the company's current position in its respective industry.

These were the contents included in an annual report. Next, we will be discussing about the financial statements.

Financial Statements:

Financial statements are one of the most important aspects of an Annual Report. They are one of the key components of the annual report and provide its users with quantitative data regarding specific aspects of its financial performance in the previous fiscal year. Financial statements come in two forms, Standalone Financial Statement and Consolidated Financial Statement. Standalone financial statement represents financials of the single company (the company itself) and do not include the financials of its subsidiaries whereas the Consolidated financial statement includes companies i.e., standalone financials and its subsidiaries financial statements. Consolidated Financial Statement gives a better representation of the company's financial position.

The 3 financial statements that will be presented by the company are:

- The Profit and Loss Statement

- The Balance Sheet and

- The Cash Flow Statement

The Profit and Loss statement is also popularly referred to as the P&L statement. It shows what happened during a time period. It contains the revenue of the company for a given period of time (usually quarterly or yearly), the expenses incurred to generate the income, taxes and depreciation, etc. While P&L statement gives us information about the profitability of the company, the balance sheet provides us with information related to assets, liabilities and shareholders' equity. P&L statement discusses the profitability for the financial year under consideration whereas Balance Sheet has financial information related to company from the time it was formed. To conclude Profit and Loss Statement shows about the performance of company in a particular financial year whereas, Balance Sheet highlights how the company has evolved financially over the years.

Now, let us discuss the Balance sheet in brief.

Balance sheet mainly consists of two components, Assets and Liabilities. Assets, whether tangible or intangible are owned by the company. An asset is a resource controlled by the company having value in monetary terms such as plants, machinery, cash, patents, land and buildings, etc. There are two types of assets, current and non-current. Current assets are the assets which are held for a period of one year whereas non-current assets are those which are held for a period more than 1 year.

Assets help the company in generating the revenues. Cash and cash equivalents of the firm are also included in assets which tells us how much the company has in its bank account.

Liability in simple words, can be considered as the loan that the company has taken and it is therefore liable to repay back. For example, short term borrowing, long term borrowing, payments due, etc. Just like assets, liabilities are also of two types, non-current and current liabilities. Non-current liabilities are the ones which the company prefers or has an intention of paying off after a time period of 1 year. On the other hand, current liabilities are those which are expected to be settled within a year. The words current and non-current in itself are enough to understand the period for which it (Assets or Liabilities) will be held.

The total assets of the company should be equal to the total liabilities of the company. The reason being, everything that a company owns has to be purchased either from the owner's capital or the liabilities. Owners' Capital is also known as "Shareholders' equity". It is the difference between Assets and Liabilities.

The total shareholders' fund is a sum of share capital and reserves and surplus. We will understand about share capital and reserves and surplus one by one with an example.

Consider a company ABC Ltd issuing shares for the first time. It issues 10,000 shares with each share having a face value of Rs. 10 each.

Here, the share capital would be Rs. 10 x 10,000 shares = Rs.1,00,000. Therefore, **Share Capital = Face Value * Number of shares**.

Reserves are generally money kept aside by the company for specific purposes and **Surplus** refers to the amount of retained earnings (Profits) of the company. Some types of reserves are Capital Reserves, General Reserve and Securities Premium reserve. Capital reserve is the money kept aside for long term projects; General Reserve is where all the profits accumulated by the company but which is not yet distributed to the shareholders reside. The premium above the face value of shares is kept under Securities Premium Reserves.

Now, you might be able to read the P&L Statement and Balance sheet or at-least get an idea about what lies in these statements. moving further we will discuss about the Cashflow statement.

The Cashflow statement is as important as the other two statements discussed earlier. You might've got a hint about what the cashflow statement deals with. To sum up in simple words, it is a statement which deals with the transactions carried out in cash, cash outflows (Expenses) and cash inflows (Income), from various activities. It shows how much the company is generating in cash. If you have read carefully up to this point you might say that the earnings are already recorded in the P&L statement, then why should we record it again? We will discuss this with the help of an example.

Consider a shop which sells designer Suits. For simplicity, let us assume that the price of each Suit is fixed at Rs.10,000. The shop sold 20 suits on a particular day amounting the total earning of the day to Rs.2,00,000. This total earning is the amount that will be shown in P&L statement. But out of the suits sold, 5 suits were sold on credit (a credit sale is when customer buys the product first and pays the amount at a latter point in time). So, the total cash sale amounts to Rs.1,50,000.

This amount which is received as cash should be recorded in cashflow statement as it will show the cash available with the company.

A cashflow statement reveals important information such as true cash position of the company, its ability to pay debt.

To sum up, every company's financial performance is dependent on liquidity or cash flows more than the profits earned during the year.

A brief on financial statements:

We have discussed the three important financial statements of the company. While the P&L and Cashflow statement are prepared on a standalone basis, representing the financial position for the given year, the Balance Sheet is prepared on a flow basis.

The P&L statement discusses the income and expenses of the company. The retained earnings of the company also called the surplus of the company are carried forward to the balance sheet.

The Balance Sheet shows the assets and liabilities of the company. On the liabilities side of balance sheet, the company represents the shareholders' funds. The total of assets and liabilities should always be equal. The balance sheet is said to be balanced when the total of assets and liabilities is equal. The cash and cash equivalents of the firm which is one of the key details of the balance sheet comes from the cashflow statement.

The cashflow statement provides information about entity's ability to generate cash and cash equivalents. It also indicates the cash needs of a company. The final number of cash flow tells us how much money the company has in its bank account after all the expenses.

You might have understood that all the three financial statements are interconnected with each other.

Next, we will discuss about some of the important ratios which are calculated with the help of these financial statements. But before that, the one thing you could do is try to read the financial statements of some companies.

Financial Ratios help in interpreting the results and allow comparison with previous years and other companies in the same industry. But the financial ratios convey very little information on its own. The ratio makes sense only when you compare the ratio with another company of a similar size or when you look into the trend of the financial ratio. To simplify things, once the ratio is calculated it has to be analysed by comparison or tracking the ratio's historical trend to get the best possible view.

Financial ratios can be classified into different categories, namely-

- Profitability Ratios

- Operating Ratios

- Leverage Ratios

- Valuation Ratios

Profitability ratios help the analyst to measure the profitability of a company, it conveys how well the company is able to perform in terms of generating profits. Ratios under the Profitability Ratio are, EBITDA Growth (CAGR), EBITDA Margin (Operating Profit Margin), PAT Margin (Profit after Tax), PAT Growth (CAGR), Return on Assets (ROA), Return on Equity (ROE) & Return on Capital Employed (ROCE)

Operating ratios measure the efficiency at which a business can convert its assets into revenues. It helps us understand the efficiency of the management and indicate the efficiency of the company's operational activities. Some of the important operating ratios are Fixed Assets turnover Ratio, Working Capital Turnover Ratio and Total Assets Turnover Ratio.

Leverage ratios also known as Solvency ratios, measure the company's ability to sustain its day-to-day operations. Leverage ratios measure the extent to which the company uses the debt to finance growth. It helps us understand the company's long-term sustainability, keeping its obligation in perspective. Some Leverage Ratios are Interest Coverage Ratio, Debt to Equity Ratio & Debt to Asset Ratio.

Valuation ratios help us in analysing whether the current share price of the company is high or low. In simpler terms, the valuation ratio shows the relationship between the market value of a company or its equity and some fundamental financial metric (e.g., earnings). Some important valuation ratios are Price to Sales Ratio, Price to Earnings (P/E) Ratio & Price to Book Value Ratio

Let us discuss these ratios in short.

The Ratios:

Now, we will be discussing about the importance of the ratios with the help of examples but not about their formulas or other technicalities involved as it is a broader concept in itself. We will discuss the ratios in detail some other time. So, without wasting any time let's get started.

Profitability ratios: -

Earnings before Interest Tax Depreciation & Amortisation (EBITDA) Margin tells us how efficient the company's model is. It tells us about the profitability of the company at an operating level in terms of percentage terms. Consider a company having an EBITDA of Rs.635 crores and its operating revenue is Rs.5500 Crs, this means that the company has retained Rs.635 Crs from its operating revenue. This same calculation if done in percentage terms, the percentage of amount retained will be known as EBITDA Margin. In this case, the company spent 88.45% of its revenue towards its expenses and retained 11.55% of the revenue at the operating level for its operation. But this information can only provide little information on its own as discussed earlier. If we compare it with the competitors or see the past trend then it will make some sense. By doing so, we can tell whether the EBITDA Margin is growing over the years or not, if it is growing then it is good for the company and we can also get an idea if it is less than the competitors or not, if EBITDA Margin of a company is greater than the peers then it is a positive news for the company.

The Profit After Tax (PAT) margin is calculated at the final profitability level. When we calculate the PAT margin, all expenses such as depreciation, finance costs and taxes are deducted from the Total Revenues of the company to identify the overall profitability of the company. Suppose, the overall revenue of a company is Rs.6000 Crs and its PAT is Rs.735 Crs. This means its PAT margin is 12.25% (PAT/Overall Revenue).

The Return on Equity (ROE) is very important ratio, as it helps the investor to assess the return the shareholder earns for every unit of capital invested. It measures the ability of the company to generate profits from shareholders' investments. The higher the ROE, the better it is for the shareholders. The average ROE of top Indian Companies ranges between 14% to 16%. If the ROE is high, it means a good amount of cash is being generated by the company. Thus, a higher ROE indicates a higher level of management performance. But with an additional debt, the ROE rises quite significantly. For example, a company acquires an asset worth 1 lakh, without any external debt, which results into an asset worth 1 lakh and shareholders' equity of 1 lakh, which balances the balance sheet. If the company generates profit of Rs.21,000 then the ROE is 21% (21,000/1,00,000 * 100).

Now consider, the company only has Rs.50,000 and borrows Rs.50,000 from his friend. This means the company's liability side would have Shareholder Equity of Rs.50,000 & a debt of Rs.50,000. In this case, ROE shoots up to 42% i.e., 21,000/50,000 * 100. This makes it clear that higher the debt, higher is the ROE. A high ROE is great but not at the cost of high debt. So, you should also look out for the debt of company too.

Return on Assets (RoA) refers to the effectiveness of the entity's ability to use the assets to create profits. Needless to say, the higher the RoA, the better it is.

The Return on Capital Employed (ROCE) indicates the profitability of the company taking into consideration the overall capital it employs. Overall capital includes both equity and debt (long term and short term). For example, a company has a PBIT (Profit before interest & taxes) of Rs.540 Crs and overall capital employed of Rs.1700 Crs. Hence, the ROCE = 540/1700 * 100 i.e., 31.76%

Operating Ratios: -

Fixed Assets Turnover Ratio tells us how effectively the company uses its fixed assets which include property, plant and equipment, etc. It measures the extent of the revenue generated in comparison to its investment in fixed assets. If the ratio is high then it means the company is efficiently and effectively utilizing its fixed assets.

The Working Capital Turnover Ratio indicates how much revenue the company generates for every unit of working capital (Working capital refers to the capital required by the firm to run its day-to-day operations). Suppose the ratio is 3, then it indicates that the company generates Rs.3 in revenue for every Rs.1 of working capital. Higher the ratio, the better it is.

The ratio which indicates company's capability to generate revenues with the given amount of assets is known as *Total Asset Turnover Ratio*. A higher total asset turnover ratio in comparison with its historical data and competitor data means the company is using its assets efficiently to generate more sales.

Leverage Ratios: -

The Interest Coverage Ratio also referred to as the debt service ratio helps us understand how much the company is earning relative to the interest burden of the company. It helps us interpret how easily a company can pay its interest payments. For example, ratio of 1.5 times means for every Rupee of interest payment due the company generates earnings of 1.5 times. A low-interest coverage ratio could mean a higher debt burden and a greater possibility of bankruptcy or default in repayment.

The Debt-to-equity ratio measures the amount of total debt capital with respect to the total equity capital. A ratio lower than 1 indicates bigger equity base with respect to debt. If the ratio is higher i.e., more than 1 then you should be careful.

Debt to asset ratio tells us how much of the total assets are financed through debt capital. Higher the percentage of this ratio, higher is the leverage and risk. Investors should be concerned if this ratio is high.

Valuation Ratios: -

Price to Sales Ratio (P/S) compares the stock price of company with the company's sales per share. For example, a P/S ratio of 2 times indicates that, for every Rs.1 of sales, the stock is valued Rs.2 times higher. The higher the ratio, the higher is the valuation of the firm.

Price to earnings (P/E) ratio is one of the most popular financial ratios. You also might have heard it many times. It indicates how expensive or cheap the stock is trading. A higher P/E ratio means the stock is expensive. Never buy stocks that are trading at high valuations. If we divide the current market price with EPS, we get the P/E ratio. P/E ratio measures the willingness of the market participants to pay for the stock, for every rupee of profit that the company generates.

The Price to Book value (P/BV) ratio indicates how many times the stock is trading over and above the book value of the firm. The higher the ratio, the more expensive the stock is which indicates the firm is overvalued relative to the equity or book value of the company and vice versa.

Make sure to compare the ratios to the past trend of the company or to its competitors to get a better idea.

With this we come to an end of this topic of Fundamental Analysis. We will now proceed to our next topic and learn about Technical Analysis.

Technical Analysis (TA): -

Technical and Fundamental analysis are the techniques which are different but not comparable. They both have their own merits and demerits. They both go hand in hand. One should try educating him/herself on both the techniques which can help in identifying great investing or trading opportunities. Technical analysis helps us to not only develop a view on the stock or index whether it will go up or down but also define the trade variables such as entry, exit, risk and reward.

Most people think that TA is a quick and easy way to make gains in the markets. But in reality, it is opposite of that. Yes, one can make handsome gains using TA but only if you do it in a right way and for that to happen one has to put in the required effort to learn the technique.

Technical Analysis is best used to identify short term trades. For long term investments you can use TA to identify the entry and exit points but you should not make long term investments purely based on TA. Long term investments are best when made using FA.

As TA based trades are usually short term in nature one should not expect huge returns within a short duration of time. One should be able to identify frequent short-term trades which can give small but consistent profits to be successful with TA. These trades which are based on TA can last anywhere between a few minutes and few weeks, and usually not beyond that. Traders enter a trade for some gains with a predefined Risk per trade i.e., Risk to Reward ratio (more on this later). Traders start to make loss when the trade starts to move against their view. Many traders keep on holding into the loss-making trade with a hope that they can recover the loss which most of the time results into even bigger loss. Remember, one should cut their losses short and hold onto the winning trades and not the other way around.

TA involves study of candlesticks, chart patterns, trends and various indicators. It can be used on any of the trading assets such as stocks, commodity, currencies, etc. which is not the case in FA. For different assets FA can be different such as analysing rainfall, demand, supply, etc. for commodities. Whereas, the concept of TA remains the same irrespective of the asset. For example, a volume indicator or Exponential Moving Average (EMA) is used in exactly the same way on stocks, commodity or currency.

While using FA one has to look at various components such as if the stock is overvalued or undervalued, its profitability, etc. whereas when using TA, the only thing that matters is the stock's past trading data (price and volume), using which we can make decisions about its future behaviour.

Some important assumptions on which technical analysis is based on are as follows: -

Markets discount everything: As we have discussed earlier in this book, the stock price reacts to any news or events which either are known or unknown in the public domain. Consider this, there could be a situation where the large institutions knew about the positive news before it was released in the market or an insider in the company buying the company's stock in large quantity in anticipation of a good quarterly earnings announcement which will be reflected already in the price meaning a good time for buying opportunity and a further up move in the stock price. (Do note that insider trading is illegal).

The "HOW" is more important than "WHY":   Continuing with the same example used above, if you see a big white candle with high volume as a result of an institutional buyer then as a technical analyst you won't be interested in why the stock was bought but you will be interested in how the price reacted to the actions of these buyers.

Let us discuss this with the help of some charts.

Have a look at chart 4.7, of **Tata Power**:

Chart 4.7

You can see that there was buying in Tata Power with high volumes leading to a big move of more than Rs.100 (From Rs.151 to Rs.255) in 12 days. Here, you will be interested in how the price reacted at the given time and not why it did so.

There are the two more important assumptions which are as follows:

Price moves in trend: Once the trend is established, the price moves in the direction of the established trend whether uptrend or downtrend. All significant moves in the market are result of a trend. Do note the price does not move in any direction continuously. In an uptrend the price moves up then there is a small pullback and then again price continues to move up.

Have a look at chart 4.8, of **TATA STEEL** below to get a better idea.

Chart 4.8

In the chart above you can see how the price moves in an uptrend, there is an impulsive move upside followed by a small correction/pullback followed by another impulsive move. This move is opposite when the price is in a downtrend.

History tends to repeat itself: The price trend tends to repeat itself. This happens because the market participants react to price movements in a remarkably similar way.

To conclude, fundamental analysis involves reading the statements of the company whereas, technical analysis involves reading the chart of the company which shows price data of the company. FA is the study of ratios, profit statements and balance sheet and TA is the study of candlesticks, trendlines, support & resistance and chart patterns.

I hope you understood the importance of Fundamental and Technical analysis and various concepts related to them. In the upcoming chapters we will be discussing about candlesticks, trendlines, support & resistance and chart patterns one by one.

5. LEARNING ABOUT THE CANDLESTICKS

To give you a background check, Candlestick trading has been around for more than four centuries which was developed by a Japanese rice trader. Candlestick signals informs us about the trading activity and overall view of other traders or investors in that particular stock or market. Candlestick signals work with all trading segments whether they are applied to commodities, stocks or futures. It doesn't matter if the market is the Nasdaq, the German DAX or the Nifty. You can trade in any of these markets using candlesticks charting system. The market speaks in the its own way which can be read using candlesticks. These candlestick signals are tried and tested for over four centuries which clears the doubt related to its reliability as something which is not reliable would not have sustained for so long.

But what exactly is a Candlestick? A candlestick consists of two parts a "The Body" and "The Shadows / Wick". A single candle includes 4 data points which are, open, high, low and close prices. It represents the trading activity in a particular stock, commodity or other segment in which trading is carried out during the particular timeframe. Timeframe can be 15 minutes, one hour, one day, one week, one month or whatever the trader prefers. A 15-minute candle will show the open, high, close and low price for 15 minutes only (For example 9:30 to 9:45). If the timeframe is one day, then a single candle represents the open, high, close and low price for a day, so on and so forth. (More on timeframes latter).

The Body: It is the part between opening price and closing price of a particular stock. When the day's opening price is lower than the closing price, the colour of the body is white. White candles represent bullishness hence can be called as bullish candles. On the other hand, when the opening price is higher than the closing price, the colour of the body is Black. Black candles represent bearishness hence can be called as bearish candle.

The Shadows/ the wick: The upper shadow or the upper wick is the line above the body and the lower shadow or the lower wick is the line below the body. In case of a white candle, the upper wick is between closing price and the highest price of the day, and the lower wick is between opening price and the lowest price of the day. In case of a black candle the upper wick is from day's open price to its high price and the lower wick is from day's closing price to the low price of that day.

Look at the following figures to understand a candle better.

In the figure 5.1, the white candle represents a bullish candle as day's opening price was lower than the closing price of the day.

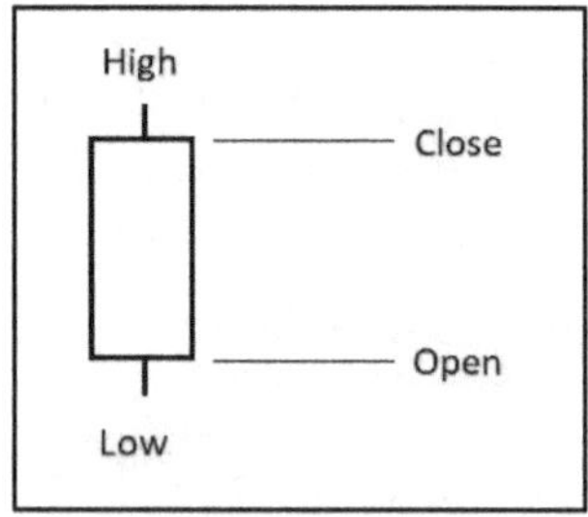

Figure 5.1

The figure 5.2 on the next page, shows a bearish candle represented by black colour. Here you can see that the opening price of the day is higher than day's closing price.

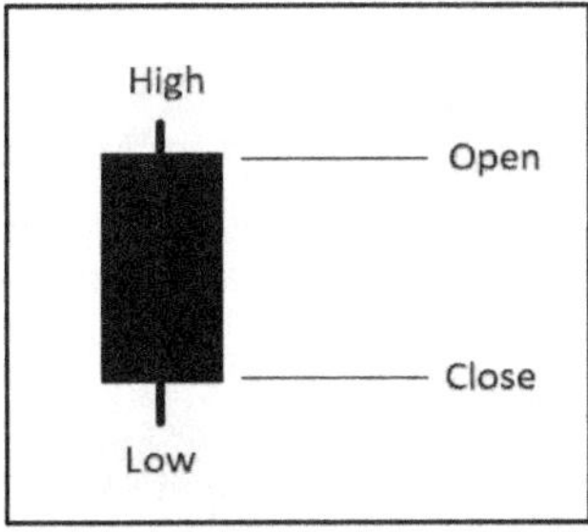

Figure 5.2

In the previous two figures (5.1 & 5.2) you can see that both the candles have both upper as well as lower wicks but it is not necessary for a candle to have both upper and lower wicks. It can have only lower wick or only upper wick or no wick at all. A candle without any wick is known as "**Marubozu**", a Japanese word meaning bald. Black and white Marubozu are those having no wicks at all. An opening marubozu does not have a wick at its opening price end of the body whereas, a closing marubozu does not have a wick at its closing price end of the body.

(Do note the colour of the candles can be different in some charting services, i.e., Green instead of White and Red instead of black).

Now, consider an example where open=Rs.105, high=Rs.120, close=Rs.120 and low=Rs.100

In this case there will be no upper wick as the closing price is equal to the high price of the day. This will also be a Closing Marubozu. So, the candle will be as shown in the figure 5.3 on the next page:

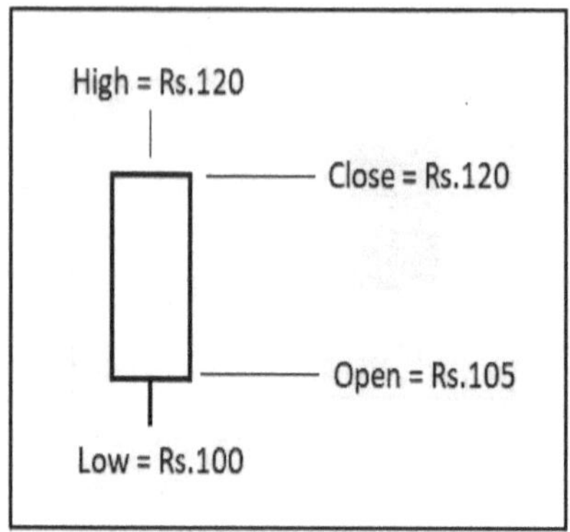

Figure 5.3

Now imagine, a situation where open=Rs.510, high=Rs.520, close=Rs.490 and low=Rs.490. Here, there won't be a lower wick as the close is equal to the low price of the day. You might've even guessed what the candle would look like in this situation.

This is also a Closing Marubozu (Figure 5.4):

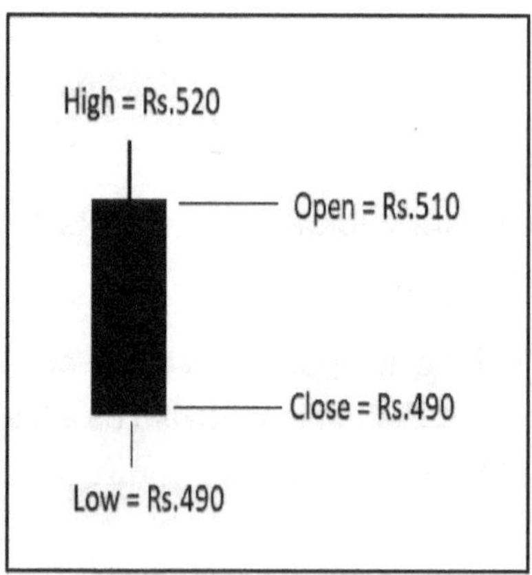

Figure 5.4

I hope you understood what a candlestick means. We will now discuss about some of the most important candlestick signals.

Types of candlestick signals:

Bullish Engulfing:

This signal is formed when a subsequent white body of a candle completely engulfs/covers the previous black candle. This signal can be considered valid only if the stock has been in a downtrend and the next day a white candle is formed engulfing the previous day black candle (the previous day candle can also be a doji), there is increase in volume on either of the two trading days. When this signal occurs, it means that the bears have lost their control and bulls have taken over. It also means that the stock is ready for trend reversal.

Look at figure 5.5 below depicting a bullish engulfing signal.

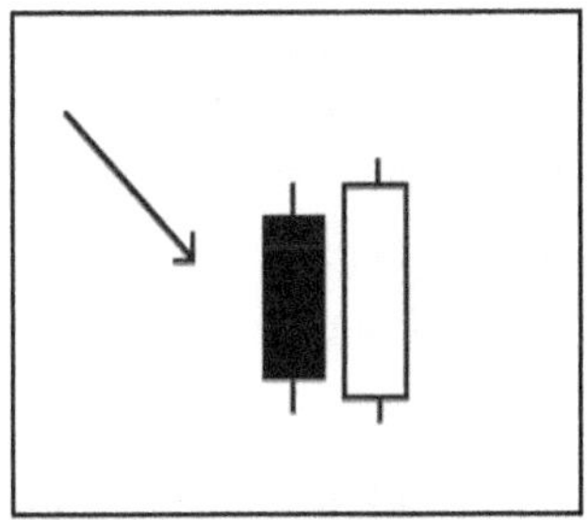

Figure 5.5

Bearish Engulfing:

This signal is formed when a subsequent black body of a candle completely engulfs/covers the previous white candle. This signal can be considered valid only if the stock has been in an uptrend and the next day a black candle is formed engulfing the previous day white candle (the previous day candle can also be a doji), there is spike in volume on either of the two trading days. When this signal occurs, it means that the bulls have lost their control and bears have taken over. It also means that the stock is ready for trend reversal.

Look at figure 5.6 below showing a bullish engulfing signal.

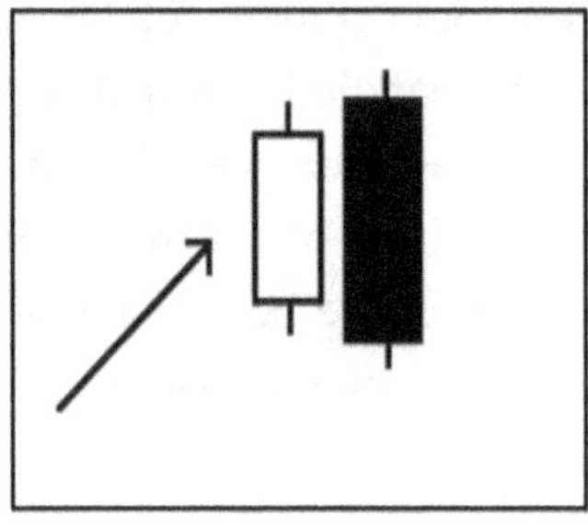

Figure 5.6

The Doji:

"Doji" is one of the most important candlestick signals. For a candle to be a doji, the open and the close of the stock must be almost at the same price level. The candle can have an upper wick or a lower wick, or both. Consider doji as an indecision in the market.

When the Doji has a small body, it is also known as a "Spinning Top".

When the Doji has only upper wick and no lower wick, it is termed as a "Gravestone Doji". If this type of doji is formed at the top of a trend it is very effective, which means that the bulls tried to rally the stock but failed at the end of the day.

A Doji without any upper shadow is known as a "Dragonfly Doji". Formation of this type of doji at the bottom of a trend means that the bears tried to pull the price down but failed at the end of the day and the bulls were able to bring the price back to where it had opened. The colour of a doji doesn't matter it can be black or white, but the one thing that matters the most is the place of occurrence of a doji.

If a doji is seen **at the top** after an uptrend, it means that the bears are fighting back to the point where bulls are unable to move the price much higher from the open and if the price opens lower the next day, there is high chance that the trend has reversed for a while.

In case of a doji appearing **after being in a downtrend** for a while, it implies that the bulls are fighting against bears and trying to move the price up and if the price stays positive on the next day, the trend reverses as the bears are nervous and have lost their control.

When a stock has been moving **sideways** for a while and then one day a big doji is formed, we will be waiting for a gap up or gap down opening the next day. This means that a trend will start in the direction of the gap. The Japanese say that a Doji at a top warrants immediate selling, but a Doji at the bottom of a trend needs confirmation of strength from the bulls. However, you can also wait for confirmation at the top. Figure 5.7 might provide you a better understanding.

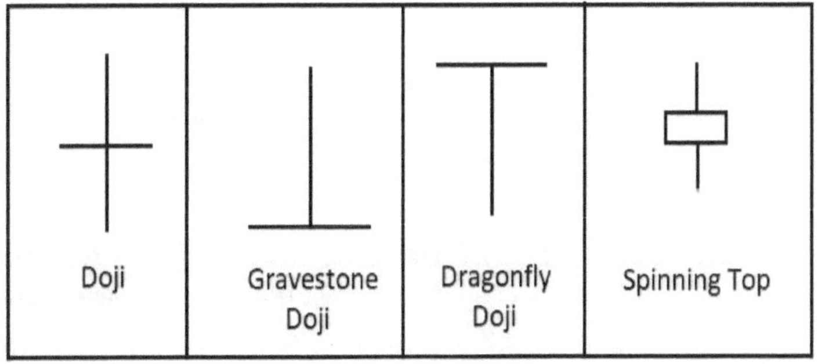

Figure 5.7

Hammer and Hanging Man:

These two signals look exactly the same, each having a small body and a tail/lower wick which is at least twice the size of the body with no upper wick or very small upper wick, the only difference is the place of their occurrence. If this signal occurs after a downtrend it is called "The Hammer" and if the signal occurs after an uptrend, it is termed as "The Hanging Man". The colour of the body doesn't matter. Also do remember one thing, the longer the tail, the better.

In the case when **The Hammer** signal is formed, it implies that the sellers are beginning to lose their grip and buyers are trying to take control. Although the colour of body doesn't matter, a white body is more positive than a black body. If the stock trades higher the next day, it means that the bulls have reversed the trend.

Look at figure 5.8, showing the hammer signal:

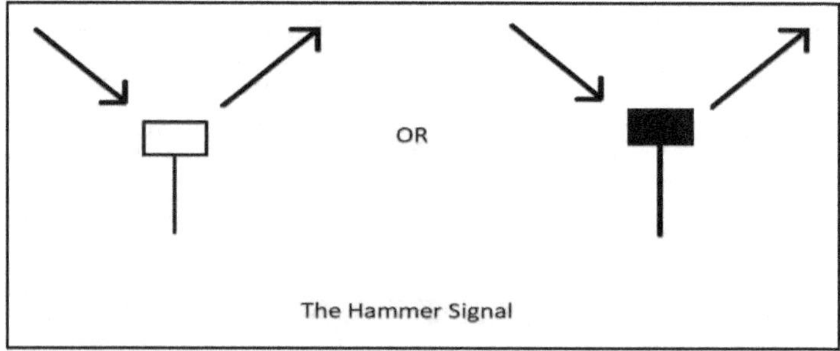

Figure 5.8

On the other hand, when the **Hanging Man** signal is formed, it means that the buyers are starting to lose their hold over the stock and the sellers are about to take over. A black body would imply stronger confirmation. The stock should trade lower the next day for the downtrend to continue. This means that bears have taken control.

The hanging man signal looks something as shown in figure 5.9.

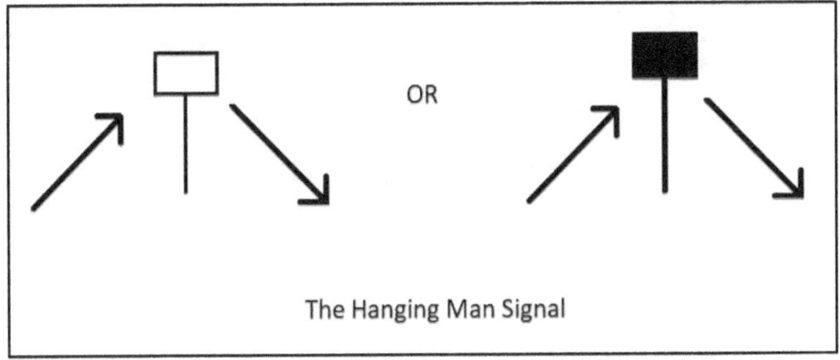

Figure 5.9

Inverted Hammer and Shooting Star:

If we flip the hammer and hanging man signals upside down, we will get Inverted hammer and Shooting star respectively, each having a small body and an upper wick which is at least twice the size of the body, without a lower wick or very small lower wick. If the signal is formed after a downtrend, it is called an "Inverted Hammer" whereas, if the signal is formed after an uptrend, it is termed as "Shooting Star". Longer the upper wick, the better it is. The colour of the body doesn't matter in these cases too.

If an **Inverted Hammer** is formed, it means that the bulls have driven the price higher during the day, but the bears pushed the price back down closing it near the open price. However, the bulls have shown their presence and if they succeed in closing the price higher the next day then it can be considered that the downtrend is broken and the trend is reversed. A white colour body refers to more positivity than black.

Have a look at figure 5.10 for better understanding:

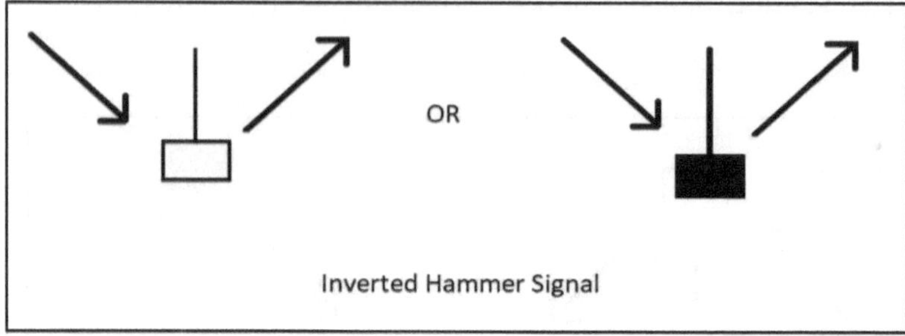

Figure 5.10

On the other hand, when a **Shooting Star** (which looks like its tail pointing to the sky) is formed, it means that the bulls tried to take the price higher but failed as bears started to show their presence by pushing the price down closing it near the open price of the day. A black colour body gives stronger confirmation than white body. If the price closes lower the day after the Shooting Star is formed, it can say that the trend is reversed. Shooting star is shown in figure 5.11:

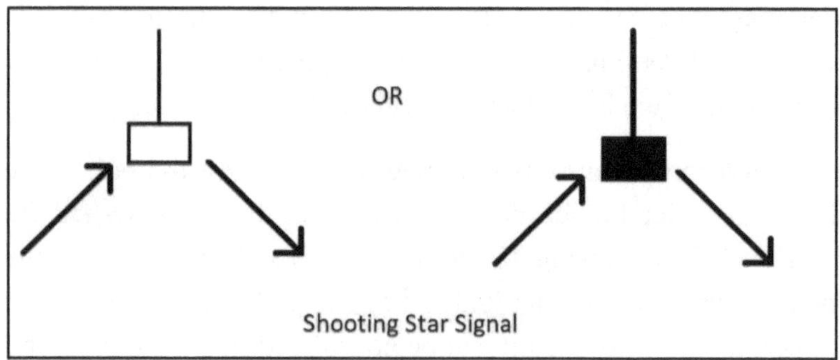

Figure 5.11

Bullish and Bearish Harami:

The word harami comes from an old Japanese word which means pregnant. The Harami occurring in an uptrend implies that the buying has stopped. In the same way, a Harami occurring in a downtrend means that the selling has stopped. If the signal occurs after a downtrend, it is known as "Bullish Harami" and if the signal is formed after an uptrend, it is termed as "Bearish Harami".

In the case of **Bullish Harami**, the 1st candle is bigger & black in colour and the next candle is small white candle which is completely engulfed by the previous day's candle. It is not necessary for the wicks of the smaller candle to be engulfed by the previous candle. The longer the black engulfing candle and the white engulfed candle, the higher the probability that the trend will be reversed.

The following figure (figure 5.12) will give you an idea about the bullish harami signal.

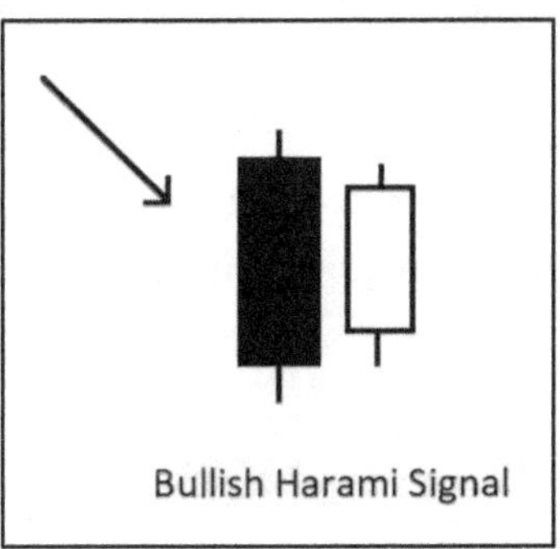

Figure 5.12

In the case of **Bearish Harami**, the 1st candle is bigger & white in colour and the next candle is small black candle which is completely engulfed by the previous day's candle. It is not necessary for the wicks of the smaller candle to be engulfed by the previous candle. The longer the white engulfing candle and the black engulfed candle, the higher the probability that the trend will be reversed.

The figure 5.13 will give you an idea about how the bearish harami signal is.

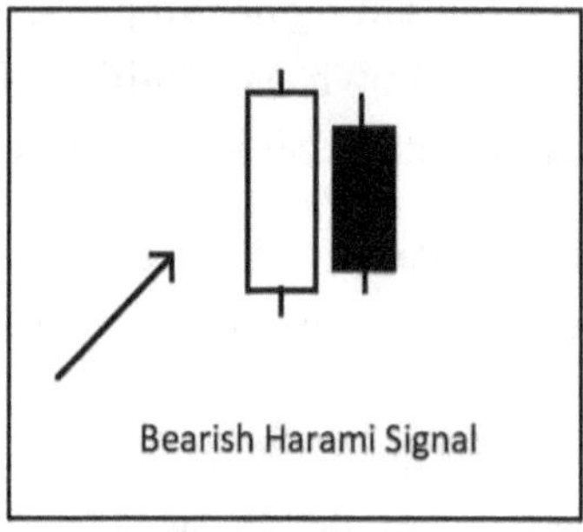

Figure 5.13

Morning Star and Evening Star:

The **morning star** is a very powerful signal which occurs after a downtrend. The first day of the signal must be a long black candle followed by a day of indecision, which means neither the bulls nor the bears are in control. The candle on third day should be a long white candle which closes at least half way into the first day's black candle. When this happens, it can be said that the stock is ready for a trend reversal. The figure 5.14 below shows what a morning star looks like.

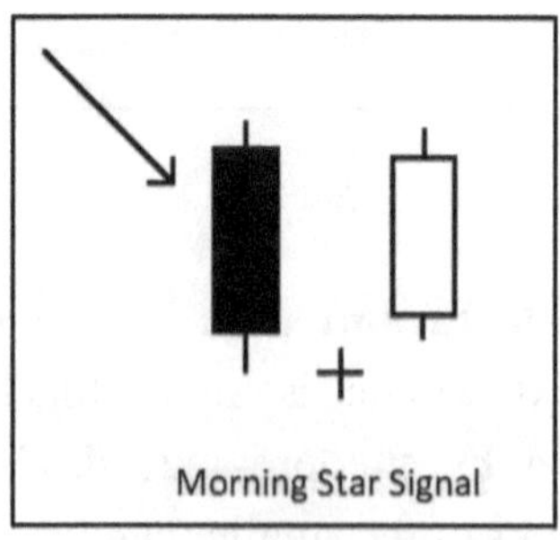

Figure 5.14

There are various types of Morning Star signal. Some of them are shown in the figure 5.15 below.

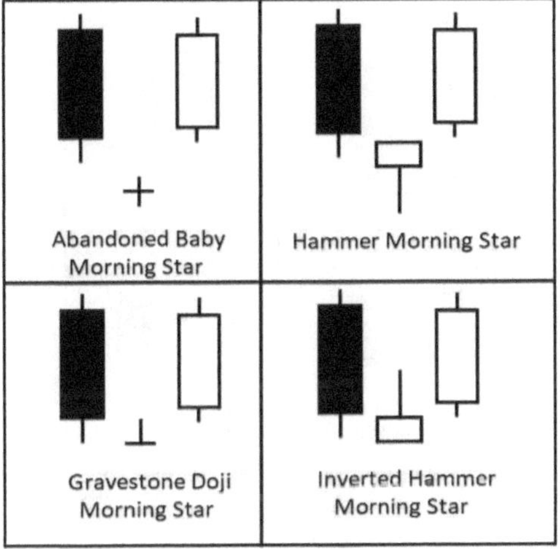

Figure 5.15

The **evening star** is also a very powerful signal which occurs after an uptrend. The first day of the signal must be a long white candle. The next day must be a day of indecision, which means the market participants are in doubt about where the price will go in near future. The third day should be a long black candle which reaches at least half way into the first day's white candle. When this happens, it can be said that the stock is ready for a trend reversal.

An evening star signal looks something like in figure 5.16 below.

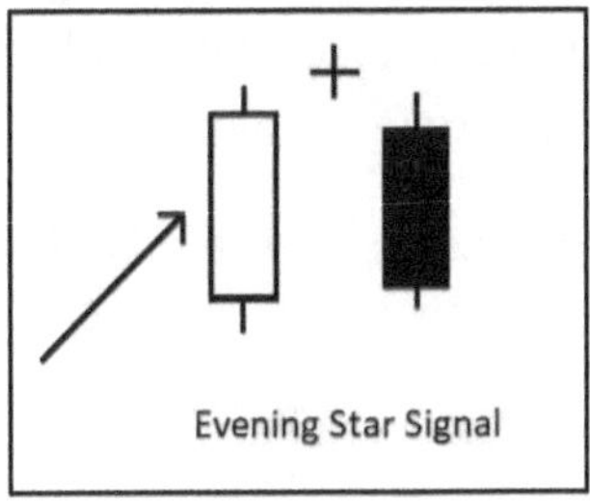

Figure 5.16

There are various types of Evening Star signal. Some of them are shown in the figure 5.17.

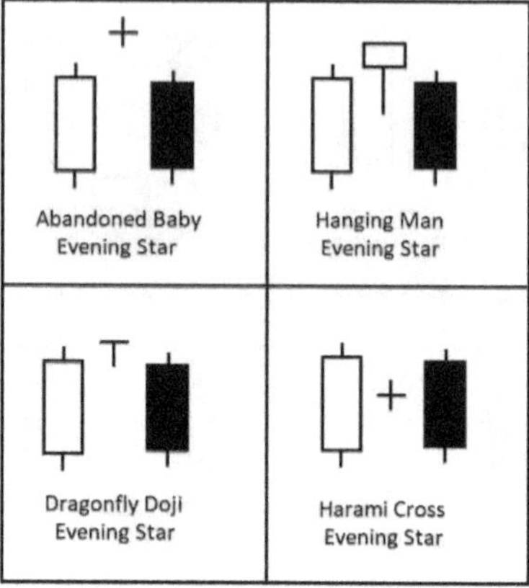

Figure 5.17

(The Abandoned baby Morning and Evening Star are considered as a very powerful signal)

Dark Cloud Cover & Piercing Signal:

A **Dark Cloud Cover signal** is formed when a black-coloured body opens above the previous day's trading range and closes more than half way into the previous day's white coloured body. This signal occurs after an uptrend.

On the second day of the signal, the candle should open above the previous white coloured body's trading range and close more than half way into it forming a black body which indicates that the trend is ready for reversal.

Figure 5.18 on the next page shows the Dark Cloud Cover Signal.

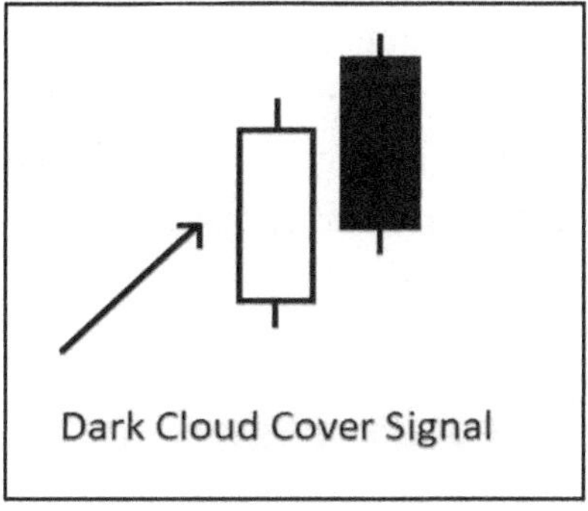

Figure 5.18

A Piercing signal is formed when a white-coloured body opens below low of the previous day's trading range and closes above the half-way point of that black body. This signal occurs after a downtrend.

On the second day of the signal, the candle should open below the previous day's black coloured body's trading range and close more than half way into it forming a white body. This means that the price trend might reverse from downtrend to uptrend.

Look at the following figure 5.19 showing Piercing Signal.

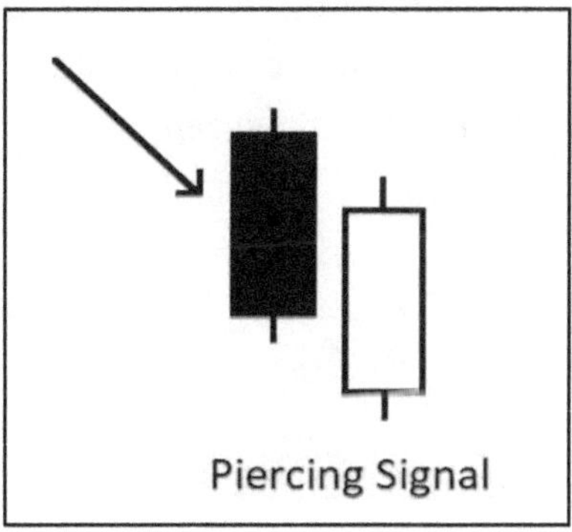

Figure 5.19

These candlestick signals mentioned above are some of the most important signals. It is absolutely fine if you don't remember the names of these candlestick signals, the only important thing to remember is what the particular candlestick signal says about the trend.

They show reversal points with a high probability. You can also use some indicators while these signals form to get an idea about the oversold or overbought condition in a particular stock and increase the probability of a successful trade. Oversold condition indicates that the stock price can rise from this point whereas, an overbought condition indicates that the price can fall from this point.

But there are going to be times when you have a perfect signal with volumes, the indicator also provides further confirmation, the signal is confirmed, you enter the trade and then the stock starts going in the opposite direction. In such situations, be wise enough to exit the trade when the stop loss hits. It is important to cut your losses short.

We will discuss about indicators, stop loss and target in the latter part of this book. But before that you should go and find these signals in the stock of your choice. Try to find as much signals as you can in various stocks so that you can easily identify the signals in the future.

6. UNDERSTANDING THE SUPPORT, RESISTANCE & TRENDLINES

Support and Resistance:

The support prevents the price from falling further as presence of buyers is more at this point. Near support level one can expect more buyers than sellers. The support level is always below Current Market Price (CMP). It is a point on the chart where traders expect maximum demand for the stock/index. Support level often acts as a trigger to buy.

The resistance is something which stops the price from rising further. The resistance price is a price at which one can expect more sellers than buyers. This level is always above the current market price. It is a point on the chart where maximum supply is expected. The resistance level often acts as a trigger to sell.

Identifying the support and resistance is very simple. If the level marked is above the CMP, it is called the resistance level and if the marked level is below the CMP, it is known as support level. To identify support, you have to draw a horizontal line on the chart below the CMP, from where the price refused to fall further and bounced back. Likewise, for resistance, you have to draw a horizontal line on the chart above the CMP, from where the price started falling, i.e., the point from which the price refused to go up.

The data points to be examined is different for finding short-term or long-term support and resistance. For short-term, one should look out for support and resistance from data of 3 to 6 months, whereas, for long-term, it should be at least 12 to 18 months (the period can vary from person to person). Support and Resistance points are more reliable if formed on a larger timeframe. Keeping the assumptions of technical analysis in mind, i.e., "History tends to repeat itself", it is believed that support and resistance points which are constructed well are usually respected.

If the support level is broken, the previous support becomes resistance whereas, if the resistance level is broken the previous resistance becomes support. For a breakout in an asset to be valid, whether downward breakout or upward breakout, the price should spend some time near the resistance or support levels, i.e., the asset should be traded near those levels for some time (consolidate). When the price breaks the levels after doing so with volumes it is a confirmed breakout and not a fake breakout. A fake breakout doesn't sustain most of the times.

Look at the highlighted points in the chart 6.1, of ITC Ltd, showing support level on daily timeframe. You can see that whenever price came near the support line it bounced back (marked with circles).

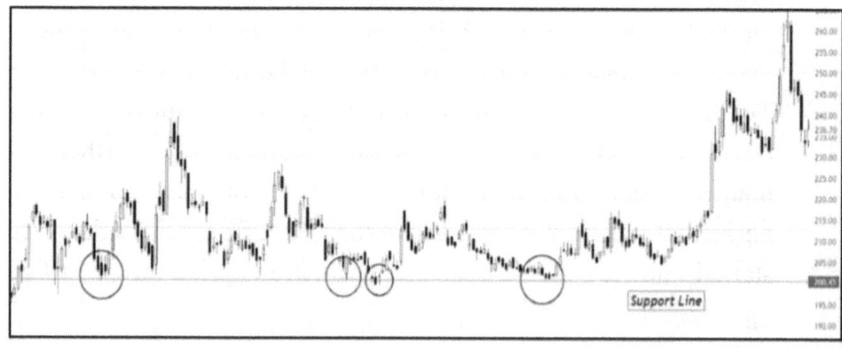

Chart 6.1

In the chart of Tata Motors below (chart 6.2), you can see that the price started falling from the marked points which acted is a resistance point:

Chart 6.2

Do note that round levels such as 100, 200, 1000, 3000, etc. also acts as support or resistance.

Trendlines:

Trendlines are easily recognizable lines that traders draw on charts to connect a series of price together. The resulting line is then used to give the trader a good idea of the direction in which an investment's value might move, i.e., up or down. These trendlines helps us to identify the prevailing direction of price. Trendlines are a visual representation of support and resistance in any time frame. They show direction and speed of price, and also describe patterns during periods of price contraction. A single trendline can be applied to a chart to give a clearer picture of the trend. The time period being analysed and the exact points used to create a trendline vary from trader to trader. Hence, trendlines can be used to help identify trends regardless of the time period, time frame or interval used.

To create a trendline, one must have at least two points on a price chart connecting each other. Some people like to use different time frames such as one minute or five minutes, some look at daily or weekly. Just like all other charting tools, trendlines also have limitations that they have to be readjusted as more price data comes in. A properly drawn trendline is respected for a long time, but sometimes the price shows more fluctuations due to which we might have to adjust the trendline. Moreover, traders often choose different data points to connect. For example, some traders will use the lowest point i.e., the wicks, while others may only use the lowest closing prices, i.e., the body. **A good trendline has multiple points touching the wicks or body of the candle.** Trendlines applied on smaller timeframes can be volume sensitive. A trendline formed on low volume may easily be broken as volume picks up throughout a session.

An ***uptrend line*** is a line drawn by connecting higher lows. It acts as support. Let us take an example to understand the concept of uptrend line connecting higher lows. Consider, a stock made a low of 100 and after some time again making a low of 110 which is higher than previous low. When these two points are connected an uptrend line is constructed as shown in the figure 6.1 below.

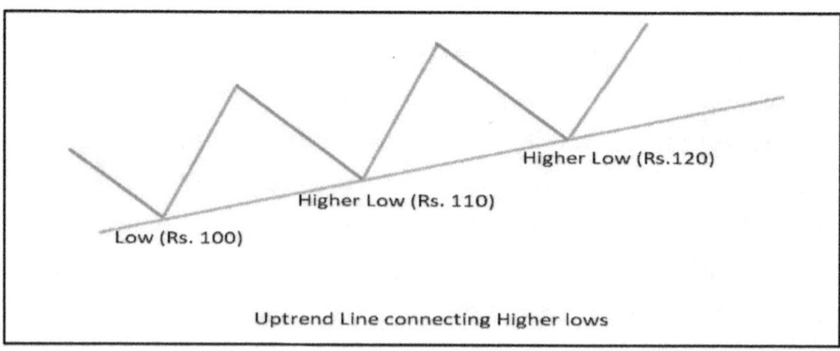

Figure 6.1

One might say why can't we connect the higher highs to form an uptrend line? It is because the price might form even higher high above the trendline made by connecting higher highs as shown in figure 6.2.

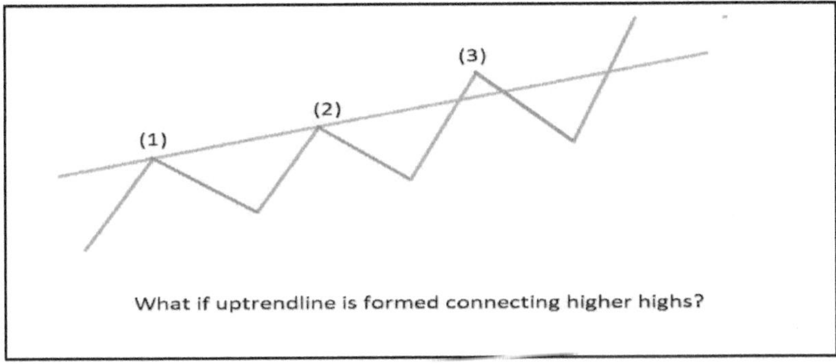

Figure 6.2

As you can see in the figure 6.2, we drew a trendline by connecting points (1) and (2) which are higher highs. But as shown above the price made even higher high, i.e., point (3), as the buying pressure is more than selling pressure. This buying pressure in the particular stock or asset doesn't let the price fall below previous low forming higher lows. Therefore, we do not construct uptrend line by connecting higher highs. However, such trendline can be used as a target.

On the other hand, a ***downtrend line*** is a line drawn by connecting lower highs. It acts as resistance. Let us take an example to understand how a downtrend line is constructed. Consider, a stock made a high of 150 and after some time again making another high of 140 which is lower than previous high. When these two points are connected a downtrend line is constructed showing that the sellers are more than buyers.

Have a look at figure 6.3 below.

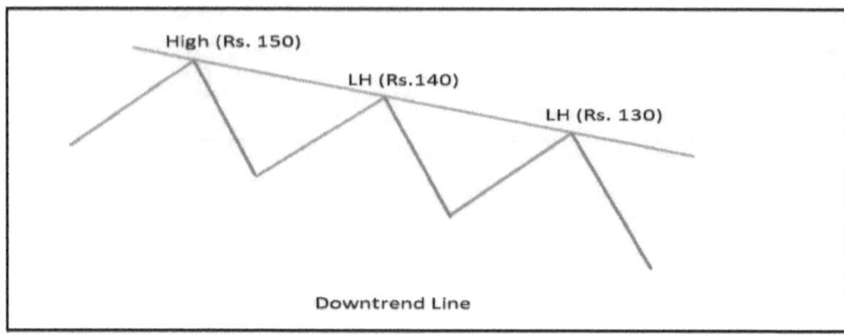

Figure 6.3

Just like an uptrend line cannot be constructed by connecting higher highs, a downtrend line also cannot be formed by connecting lower lows as the next low can be formed lower which might even break the trendline.

Have a look at charts ahead to get a better view about trendlines.

Uptrend Line:

Chart 6.3

In the chart above (chart 6.3), you can see that the line acted as support for Banknifty. The price bounced back whenever it came near the trendline respecting the uptrend line. Once the trendline was broken, Banknifty fell by more than 3,000 points.

Downtrend Line:

Chart 6.4

In chart 6.4, it can be seen that the downtrend line which is acting as resistance for the price in EXIDE INDUSTRIES was respected many times.

Adjusted Trendline:

Chart 6.5

Do note, the two points used to form a trendline should not be too far apart, or too close together. Two or three points must be connected before the line is considered to be a valid trendline. You will see that the trendlines will be respected if they are constructed properly and price will start to rise or fall again after touching the trendline. But if the price has broken the trendline we might see a reversal.

I hope you understood what the support, resistance and trendlines are. I would suggest you to try and find support, resistance and trendlines in some stocks to test your knowledge and practice as much as you can so that it can help you identify opportunities in the market.

7. THE CHART PATTERNS

The collection of various candlesticks which provides the information related to the price of the stock is known as a chart. The charts help us to understand how the price have moved over the period of time i.e., from the day it was listed on the exchange. The patterns which are formed in the charts are known as Chart patterns, as you might have guessed from the name itself.

Chart pattern analysis can be used to make short-term as well as long term forecasts and also helps in identifying trend reversals and continuations. The data used to identify the chart patterns can be intraday, daily, weekly, monthly or yearly. These patterns are a great way of looking at price actions occurring during the trading period of the stock. If you can recognize these patterns early, they will help you gain a real competitive advantage in the markets.

There are more than 30 chart patterns which suggests us what the price might do next, based on what they have done in the past. In this chapter, we will be studying about some of the most important chart patterns.

The patterns that will be discussed in this chapter are:

- Head and Shoulders

- Inverted Head and Shoulders

- Double Top & Double Bottom

- Ascending and Descending Triangles

- Symmetrical Triangles

- Falling and Rising Wedges

- Flag or pennants

Head and Shoulders:

The name has nothing to do with the shampoo brand. Head and shoulders pattern is considered to be one of the most reliable reversal chart patterns. This pattern tries to predict a bull to bear market reversal. It is a chart pattern which has a large peak with two smaller peaks either side i.e., left and right. The two smaller peaks look like the left and right shoulders whereas, the larger peak looks like a head. All the three levels fall back to the same level of support, known as the 'neckline'. Once the third peak has fallen back to the support level, it is likely that it will break the support resulting into downtrend. When this break happens, we can find selling opportunity.

Try to understand this pattern with the help of figure 7.1.

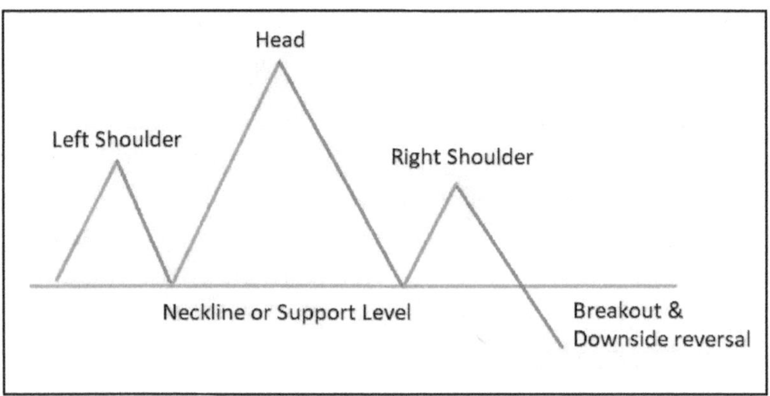

Figure 7.1

The support for head and shoulders can also be a trendline as shown in chart 7.1, of Nifty 50 Index below:

Chart 7.1

Inverted Head and Shoulders:

As the name suggests, it is the opposite of the head and shoulders pattern. This pattern tries to predict a bear to bull market reversal. In this pattern the price rises again and again to the same resistance level forming an inverted head and shoulders pattern as shown in figure 7.2. Once the third peak has reached to the resistance level, it is likely that it will break the resistance. When it breaks the resistance with volumes it will result into an uptrend. One can find buying opportunity once the price breaks the resistance.

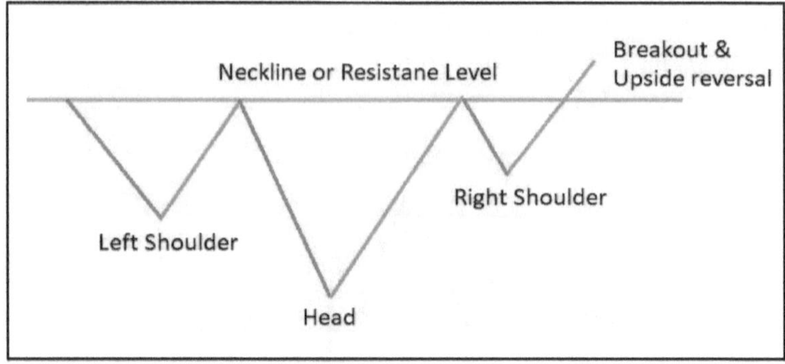

Figure 7.2

The inverted head and shoulders pattern in the HDFC Bank:

Chart 7.2

Double Top:

A double top is an extremely bearish technical reversal pattern that forms after an asset reaches a high price two consecutive times, the second high being slightly below the first top indicating resistance and exhaustion. It is also referred to as 'M pattern' because the double top has a 'M' shape. The bearish movement is confirmed once the asset's price falls below a support level equal to the low between the two prior highs. One can enter the trade once the underlying asset breaks the support level, with a stop loss just above the breakout candle.

Double Top as per theories:

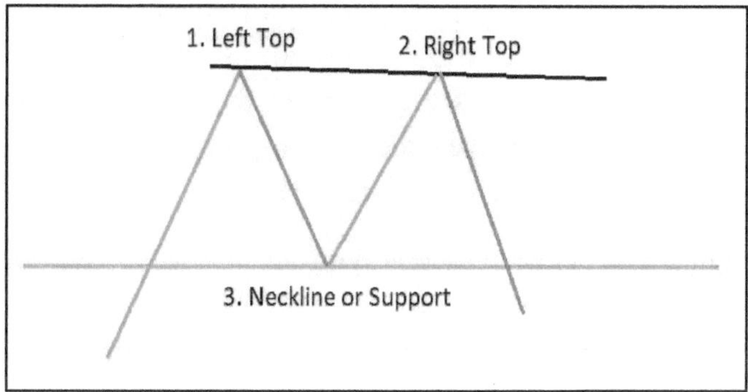

Figure 7.3

Double Top formation in Tata Power can be seen in chart 7.3. You can see that once the price broke the support level, it gave an easy target of more than 1:2.

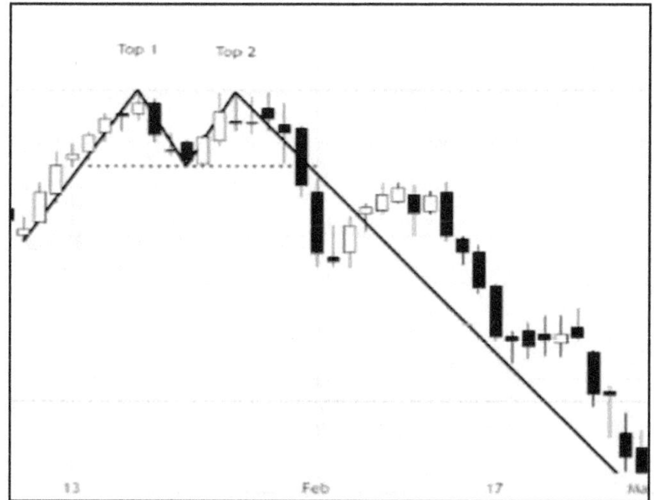

Chart 7.3

Double Bottom:

The double bottom looks like the letter 'W', therefore also referred as W 'pattern' which indicates that the price has made two unsuccessful attempts at breaking the support level. This chart pattern indicates a bullish price movement. The upward movement of price is confirmed once the asset's price breaks the resistance level equal to the high between the two prior lows. One can enter the trade once the underlying asset breaks the resistance level, with a stop loss just below the breakout candle.

The figure 7.4 below will give you an idea about the Double bottom formation.

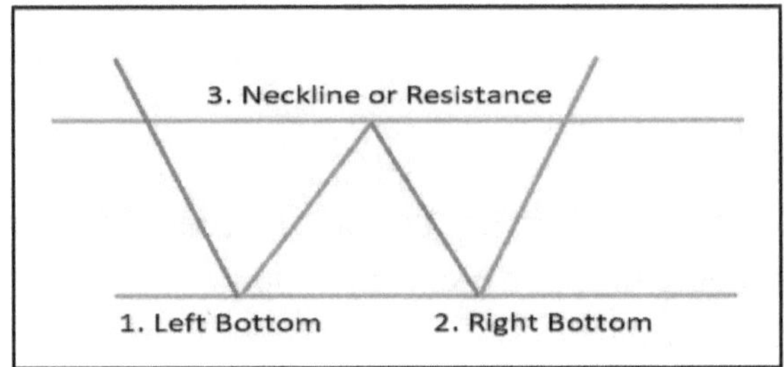

Figure 7.4

Double bottom on the charts (Chart 7.4) of INDUSIND BANK:

Chart 7.4

Ascending and Descending Triangles:

The **ascending triangle** is a bullish continuation chart pattern which signifies that a breakout is possible where the triangle lines converge. To draw this pattern, one has to place a horizontal line i.e., the resistance line, on the resistance points and draw an uptrend line along the support points connecting the higher lows. The trend line signifies the overall uptrend of the pattern, while the horizontal line indicates the level of resistance for that particular asset. Once the price breaks the resistance level, we can enter the trade in the direction of breakout with appropriate stop loss just below the breakout point.

The figure 7.5 shows what generally happens in an ascending triangle formation:

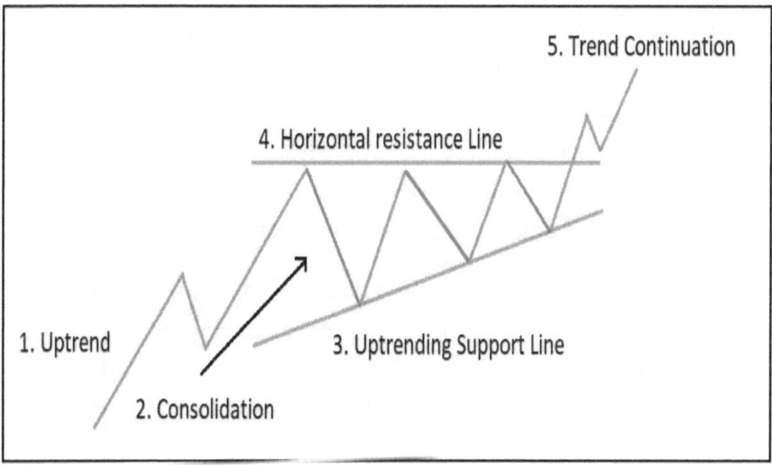

Figure 7.5

Ascending Triangle formation in CRISIL (Chart 7.5):

Chart 7.5

On the contrary, **a descending triangle** signifies a continuation of a downtrend. Generally, a trader can enter a short position during a descending triangle in order to make profit from a falling market. Descending triangles can be identified with the help of a horizontal support line and a downward-sloping resistance line formed by connecting the lower highs. In the end, the trend will break the support and continue its downtrend.

As per theory descending triangle pattern is as follows (figure 7.6)

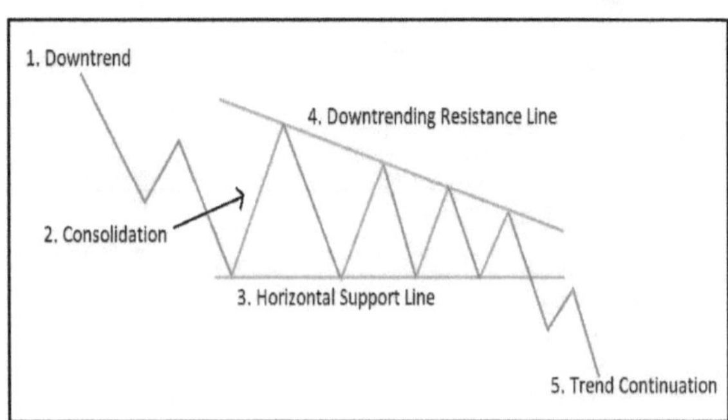

Figure 7.6

Descending triangle pattern on the chart (7.6) of INDHOTEL:

Chart 7.6

Symmetrical Triangles:

Symmetrical triangle pattern can either be bullish or bearish depending on the market. The market will usually continue in the same direction as the overall trend once the pattern has formed. Symmetrical triangles form when the price converges with a series of lower highs and higher lows. In the following example (Chart 7.7) you can see that the trend is bearish, the symmetrical triangle formation indicating a pause before falling further. As you can see, the price kept falling, giving a good target to a trader.

Chart 7.7

If there is no clear trend before the formation of this pattern, the market could break out in either direction which makes these triangles a bilateral pattern. These are best used in a volatile market where there is no clear indication of which way an asset's price might move.

Have a look at figure 7.7 for a quick overview:

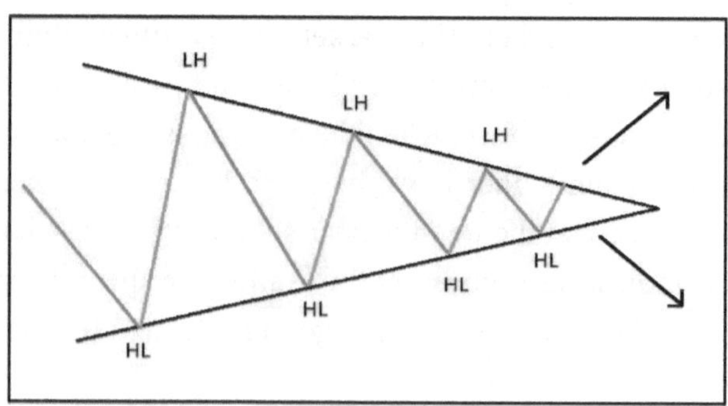

Figure 7.7

*LH=Lower High; HL=Higher Low

(The breakout can happen in any direction either up or down. However, it usually follows the trend in which the price of underlying asset is).

Wedges:

A wedge pattern is formed when the price movement of an asset tightens between the support and resistance lines. Wedge can be either a rising wedge or a falling wedge. The wedge doesn't have a horizontal trend line like the triangles, it is characterized by either two upward trend lines or two downward trendlines.

For a falling wedge, it is thought that the price will break through the resistance and for a rising wedge the price is expected to break through the support. The rising wedge represents a bearish market whereas, a falling wedge represents a bullish market. This means that the wedge is a reversal pattern as the breakout is opposite to the general trend. One can enter the trade once the support or resistance is broken with an appropriate stop loss.

Rising Wedge formation:

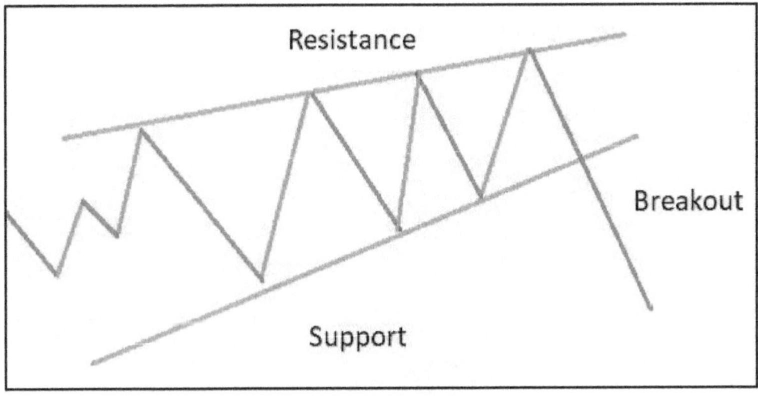

Figure 7.8

In chart 7.8, we can see a rising wedge formation in ITC:

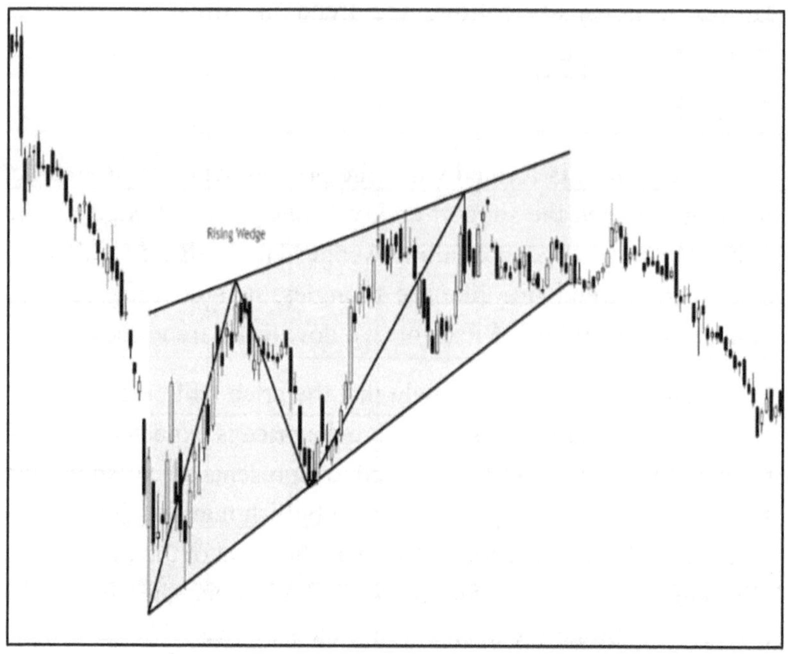

Chart 7.8

Falling Wedge formation:

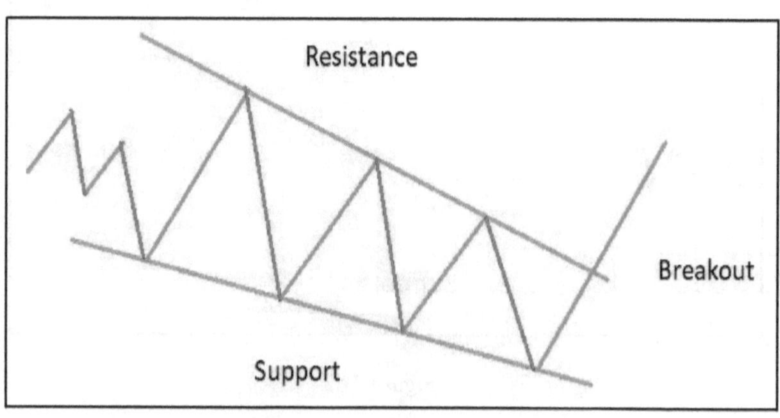

Figure 7.9

The falling wedge formation in TITAN:

Chart 7.9

Flag or Pennants:

Flag is formed when there is a minor profit booking in either an uptrend or a downtrend. In this pattern the consolidation phase is characterized by parallel trend lines. The upper trend line acts as resistance while the lower trend line acts as support. The breakout is usually the opposite direction of the trendlines.

The bullish flag formation can be found in stock with strong uptrends and are considered good continuation patterns. They are called bull flags because the pattern resembles a flag on a pole. The pole is the result of a rally in price of a stock and the flag

87

results form a period of consolidation. Consolidating in an uptrend means that the price will make a small retracement before continuing the uptrend. Have a look at the figure 7.10 showing bullish flag formation.

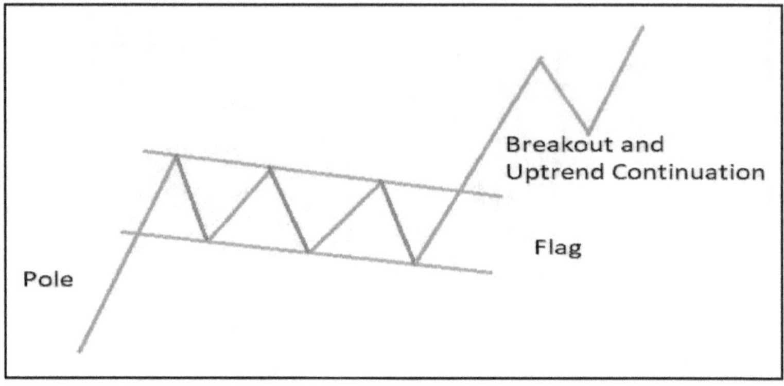

Figure 7.10

Bullish Flag formation in Reliance Industries:

Chart 7.10

The bearish flag chart pattern indicates the downtrend extension once the temporary pause i.e., consolidation phase, is finished. In the case of bearish flag formation, the price after falling sharply, makes a small pause before continuing in downtrend. The figure 7.11 shows a bearish flag formation.

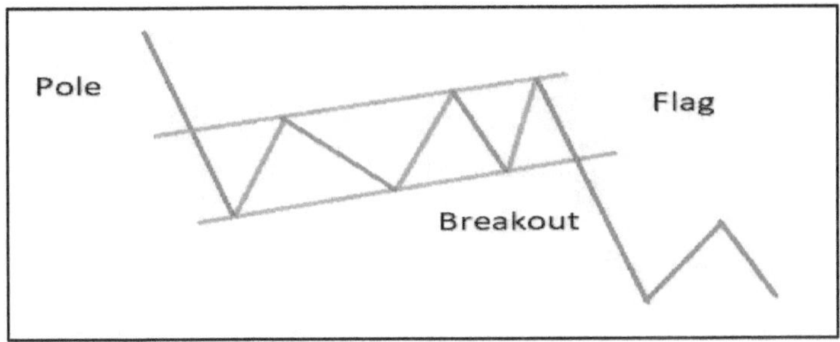

Figure 7.11

Bearish Flag Formation in HCL Technologies:

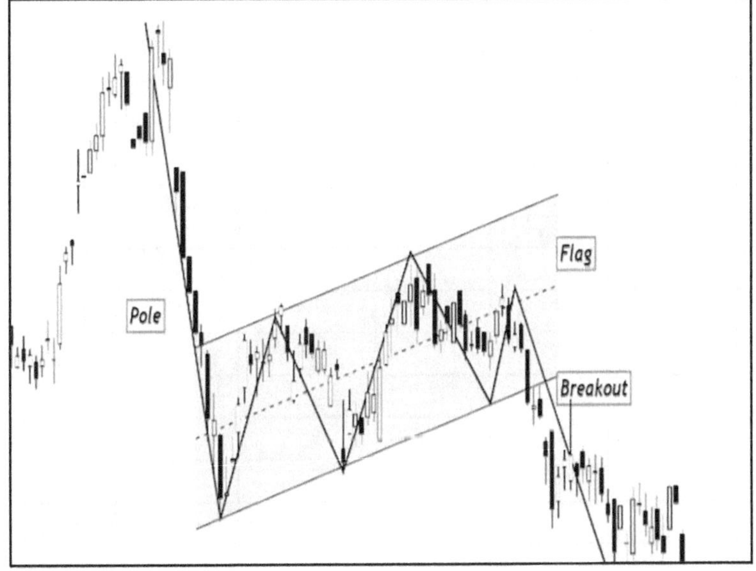

Chart 7.11

The pennant pattern is identical to the flag pattern in its setup and implications, the only difference is that the consolidation phase of a pennant pattern is characterized by converging trend lines just like in the figure 7.12 below.

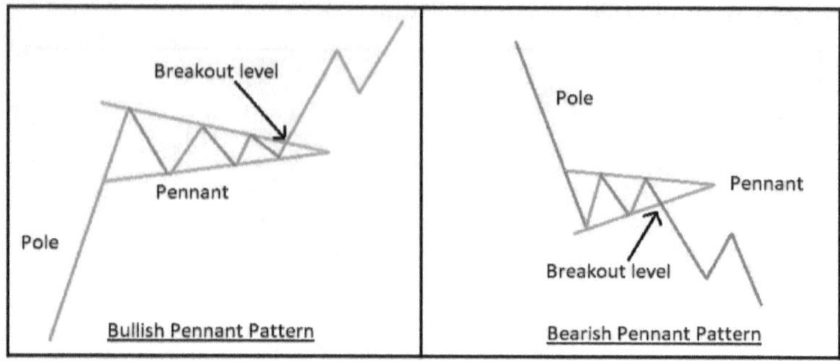

Figure 7.12

The chart 7.12 shows both bullish(Left i.e., Adani Green) and bearish(Right i.e., TCS) pennant pattern:

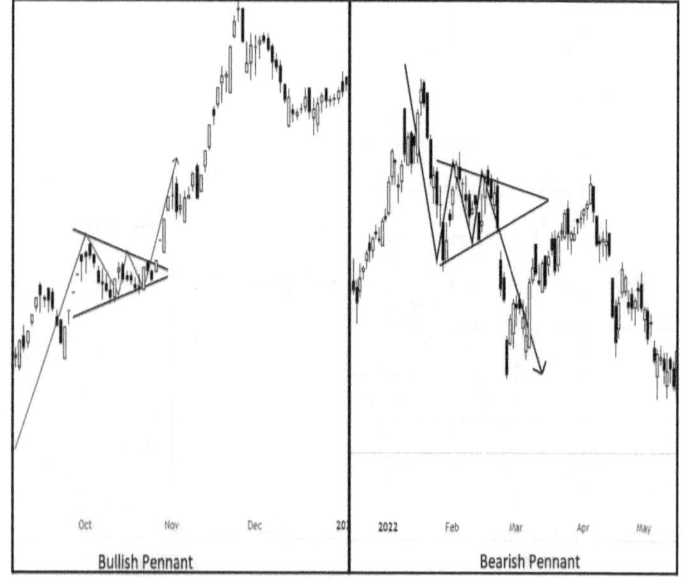

Chart 7.12

Do note, sometimes, these patterns can fail too. You can use combination of indicators to confirm the breakout in the patterns and enter the trade accordingly and always remember to enter with a stop loss.

With this, it is now time to move onto the next chapter.

8. LEARNING ABOUT THE INDICATORS

Indicators are the tools which help you to show what has happened in the past. Indicators are used along with the candlestick signals or chart patterns by the traders to confirm their view. However, it is not advisable to rely solely on the indicators to make trading decisions.

There are many indicators which are used by the traders. But we will discuss some of the most used indicators in this chapter.

Simple Moving Average (SMA):

A Simple Moving Average (SMA) also known as Moving Average, is a moving average calculated by adding recent prices and then dividing that figure by the number of time periods in the calculation average. For example, one could add the closing price of a security for a number of time periods, say 15 days, and then divide this total by that same number of periods.

SMA makes it easier for the traders to identify the price trend of the asset. If the simple moving average points up, this means that the price is increasing. If it is pointing down, it indicates that the price is decreasing. Along with identifying the trend, moving averages are also used to identify support and resistance levels in an underlying asset.

Short-term averages respond quickly to changes in the price of the underlying asset, while long-term averages react slowly. The longer the time frame for the moving average, the smoother the simple moving average. A shorter-term moving average is more volatile, but its reading is closer to the source data.

Traders also use this indicator to compare a pair of simple moving averages with each covering different time frames. The 50-day, 100-day and 200-day moving averages are most commonly used averages. The combination of 200 Day MA (Long term average) and 50 Day MA (Short term average) is mostly used of the traders. When the 50-day moving average (Short term) crosses the 200-day moving average (Long term) from below, i.e., when the short-term MA goes above the long-term MA, an uptrend is expected. This crossover is also known as "Golden Crossover".

On the other hand, when the 50-day moving average crosses the 200-day moving average from above, i.e., when the short-term MA goes below the long-term MA, a downtrend is expected. This crossover is known as "Death Crossover". (Do note, one can use any combination of averages as per their setup according to their convenience).

One major drawback of SMA's is that it may rely too heavily on outdated data since it treats the 10th or 200th day's impact the same as the first or second day.

Chart 8.1 of NESTLE INDIA shows the golden & death crossovers.

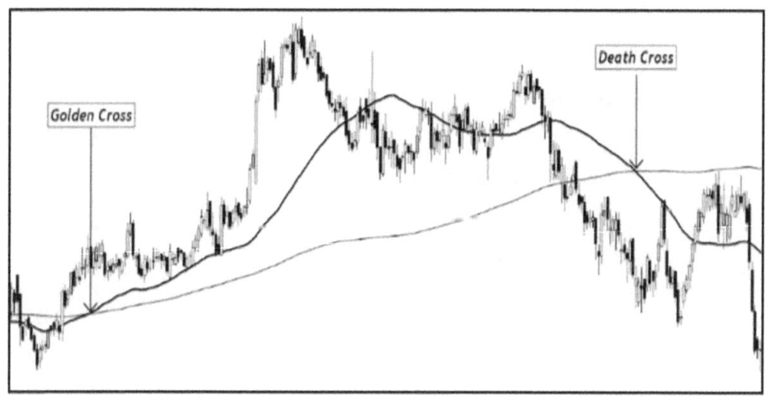

Chart 8.1

The line which is closer to the candles represents the short-term moving average, here, it indicates the 50-day MA whereas, the line which is not so close to the candles represents the long-term moving average, in the above chart it represents the 200-day MA. It is easy to identify which line is short term based and which line is based on long term as the short-term moving average lines are closer to the candles than the long-term average lines.

You can change the colour of these lines as per your preferences.

Exponential Moving Average (EMA):

The major difference between an exponential moving average (EMA) and a simple moving average is the sensitivity each one shows to changes in the data used in its calculation. Unlike SMA, the EMA gives a higher importance to recent prices.

The two averages are similar because they are interpreted in the same manner and are both commonly used by traders to smooth out price fluctuations. Many traders prefer EMAs over SMAs because EMAs give higher weightage to recent price data than older data. Due to this they are more reactive to latest price changes which makes the results from EMAs more reliable and explains why the EMA is the preferred average among many traders.

Usually, short-term exponential moving averages include the 12-day and 26-day EMA. The 50-day and 200-day exponential moving averages are used to indicate long-term trends. The concept of golden and death cross is same in both SMA and EMA.

Have a look at the chart of LUPIN LTD below (Chart 8.2) which shows the 50-day and 200-day EMA lines.

Chart 8.2

Do note that these crossovers also can fail and give a false buy or sell signal. Hence, these indicators should be used as a tool in combination with chart patterns, signals or breakouts to trade.

Relative Strength Index (RSI):

The Relative Strength Index (RSI) is used to evaluate overbought or oversold conditions in the price of a stock or other asset by measuring the recent price changes. The RSI provides traders with signals about bullish and bearish price momentum. The RSI is displayed as an oscillator (a line graph that moves between two extremes) and can have a reading from 0 to 100. An asset is usually considered overbought when the RSI is above 70% and oversold when it is below 30%. Whenever the RSI crosses the level of 30 or 70, the price might be prepared for a reversal or pullback.

During an uptrend, the RSI tends to stay above 30 and should frequently hit 70. During a downtrend, it is rare to see the RSI exceed 70, and the indicator frequently hits 30 or below. These guidelines can help determine strength in the trend and spot potential reversals.

Divergence is when the price of an asset is moving in the opposite direction of a technical indicator, such as RSI. When RSI is falling but the price is not, it is known as "Bearish Divergence". Bearish Divergence can be spotted by connecting highs on the downward trendline on RSI.

When RSI is increasing but the price is not it is "Bullish Divergence". Bullish Divergence can be spotted by connecting lows on the upward trendline on RSI.

For example, if the RSI can't reach 70 on a number of consecutive price swings during an uptrend, but then drops below 30, the trend has weakened and could be reversing. On the other side, if the downtrend is unable to reach 30 or below and then rallies above 70, that downtrend has weakened and could be reversing. Trend lines and moving averages are helpful tools to include when using the RSI in this way.

Chart 8.3 of NESTLE India (Daily TF) shows bullish divergence (RSI making higher low and price staying at same level).

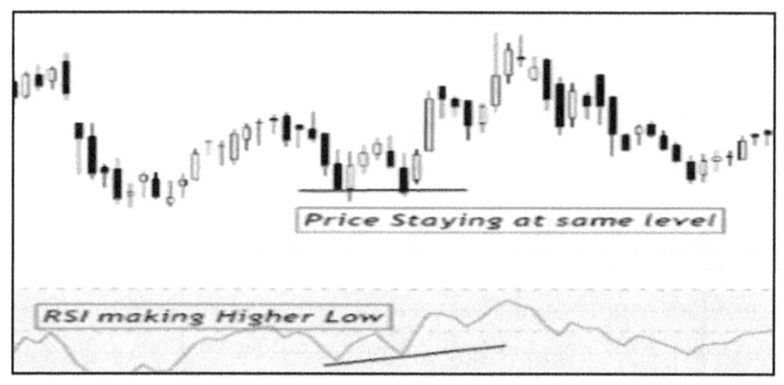

Chart 8.3

Following Chart 8.4, of JSW STEEL LTD (Daily TF) shows Bearish divergence (RSI making lower high and price making higher high):

Chart 8.4

You can clearly see from the charts above that in bullish divergence the RSI was rising but the price was not. While in bearish divergence, we can see that price was rising when RSI was falling.

Also remember, since the indicator displays momentum, it can stay overbought or oversold for a long time when an asset has significant momentum in either direction. Therefore, the RSI is most useful in an oscillating market where the asset price is alternating between bullish and bearish movements.

Fibonacci Retracement:

Fibonacci retracement levels are horizontal lines that indicate where support and resistance are likely to occur. Each level is associated with a percentage. The percentage is how much of a prior move the price has retraced. The Fibonacci retracement levels which are most commonly used are 23.6%, 38.2%, 61.8%, and 78.6%. The percentage levels provided are areas where the price could stall or reverse. However, one should not solely rely on these levels, as it is dangerous to assume the price will reverse after hitting a specific Fibonacci level.

Fibonacci retracement levels connect any two points, typically a high point and a low point. The indicator will then create the levels between those two points.

For example, consider the price of a stock rises Rs.10 and then drops by Rs.2.36. In that case, it has retraced 23.6%, which is a Fibonacci number. Fibonacci numbers are found throughout nature which you can search on the web. Therefore, many traders believe that these numbers also have relevance in financial markets.

Fibonacci retracements can be used to place entry orders, determine stop-loss levels, or set price targets. For example, a trader may see a stock moving higher. After a move up, it retraces to the 61.8% level. Then, it starts to go up again. Since the bounce occurred at a Fibonacci level during an uptrend, the trader decides to buy. The trader might set a stop loss at the 61.8% level, as a return below that level could indicate that the rally has failed.

Fibonacci retracement levels are static (that doesn't change), unlike moving averages, which allows for quick and easy identification. That helps traders and investors to anticipate and react prudently when the price levels are tested. These levels are points where some type of price action is expected, either a reversal or a break.

Chart 8.5, of EICHER MOTORS shows the Fibonacci retracement levels drawn using a low point and a high point which are highlighted.

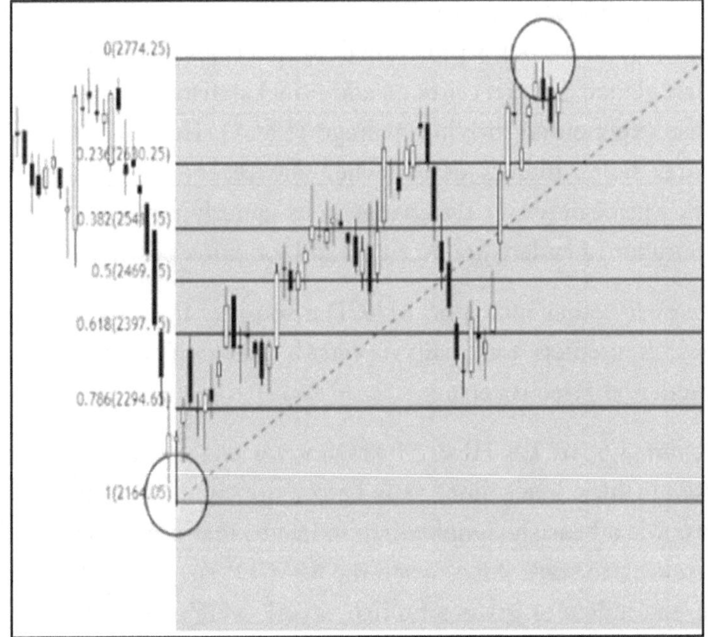

Chart 8.5

Moving Average Convergence Divergence (MACD):

Moving average convergence divergence (MACD) is an indicator that shows the relationship between two moving averages of a security's price. The "signal line" is plotted on top of the MACD line, which can function as a trigger for buy and sell signals. Traders may buy the security when the MACD crosses above its signal line and sell—or short—the security when the MACD crosses below the signal line. MACD triggers technical signals when it crosses above (to buy) or below (to sell) its signal line. The speed of crossovers is also taken as a signal of a market is overbought or oversold. MACD helps investors understand whether the bullish or bearish movement in the price is strengthening or weakening.

Basically, traders use MACD to identify changes in the direction or severity of a stock's price trend. MACD can seem complicated at first glance, since it relies on additional statistical concepts such as the exponential moving average (EMA). But fundamentally, MACD helps traders detect when the recent momentum in a stock's price may signal a change in its underlying trend. This can help traders decide when to enter, add, or exit a position.

Like every other indicator, MACD also gives false signals many times. It predicts too many reversals that don't occur and not enough real price reversals.

In chart 8.6, of EICHER MOTORS we can see that when the MACD (thick black line) falls below the signal line (thin black line), it is a bearish signal which indicates that it may be time for the selling to start. Also, when the MACD rises above the signal line, the indicator gives a bullish signal, which suggests that the price of the asset is likely to give upward momentum.

Chart 8.6

When the MACD rises or falls rapidly (the shorter-term moving average pulls away from the longer-term moving average), it is a signal that the security is overbought or oversold and will soon return to normal levels. Traders should combine this analysis with other technical indicators to verify overbought or oversold conditions.

Volume Weighted Average Price (VWAP):

VWAP is a single-day indicator and is restarted at the open of each new trading day. The volume-weighted average price (VWAP) is a trading benchmark used by traders which shows the average price a security has traded at throughout the day, based on both volume and price. It appears as a single line on intraday charts (1 minute, 15 minutes, and so on).

VWAP is important because it provides traders with insight into both the trend and value of a security. Retail and professional traders may use the VWAP as part of their trading rules for determining intraday trends. As the price breaks the support level of the VWAP it indicates a possible bearish trend, whereas, when the price breaks the resistance, the underlying asset is expected to be in a bullish trend. If the price is above the VWAP line it will act as support and if price is below the line it will act as resistance.

Traders may use VWAP as a trend confirmation tool, and build trading rules around it. For example, when the price is above VWAP, they may prefer to buy. When the price is below VWAP they may prefer to sell.

The VWAP is used by traders who wish to see a smoother indication of a security's price over time. It is also used by larger traders who need to ensure that their trades do not move the price of the security they are trying to buy or sell. For example, a hedge fund might refrain from submitting a buy order for a price above the security's VWAP, in order to avoid artificially inflating the price of that security. Likewise, it might avoid submitting orders too far below the VWAP, so that the price is not dragged down by its sale.

In chart 8.7, of State Bank of India, when the price crosses the resistance level you can see that price gave upward movement whereas, when the price breaks the support level you can see that the price started moving downwards.

Chart 8.7

Bollinger Bands:

Bollinger Band is a type of chart indicator which is widely used by traders in many markets, including stocks, futures, and currencies. The bands offer unique insights into price and volatility. These bands are used as a tool for determining overbought and oversold levels, as a trend following tool, and for monitoring for breakouts. They are a trading tool used to determine entry and exit points for a trade. However, using only the bands to trade is a risky strategy as the indicator focuses on price and volatility, while ignoring a lot of other relevant information.

It has 3 bands, upper, middle and lower. Upper and lower bands act as resistance and support respectively, whereas, the middle band is Moving average. When the price of the asset breaks below the lower band of the Bollinger Bands, it indicates that the prices have fallen too much and are due to move upwards, hence giving a buy signal. On the other hand, when price breaks above the upper band, the market is perhaps overbought and ready for a pullback, giving sell signal.

However, Bollinger Bands don't always give accurate buy and sell signals. During a strong trend, for example, the trader runs the risk of placing trades on the wrong side of the move because the indicator can flash overbought or oversold signals too soon. To solve this problem, traders can look at the overall direction of price and then only take trade signals that align with the trend. For example, if the price is in a downtrend, traders should only take short positions when the upper band is touched. The lower band can still be used as an exit point if desired, but the price touching the lower band doesn't give new buy signal as the stock is still in a downtrend.

Chart **8.8**, of KOTAK MAHINDRA BANK below, you can see how the price starts to fall after touching the upper band and rises after touching lower band. However, it may not be the case every time it touches the bands.

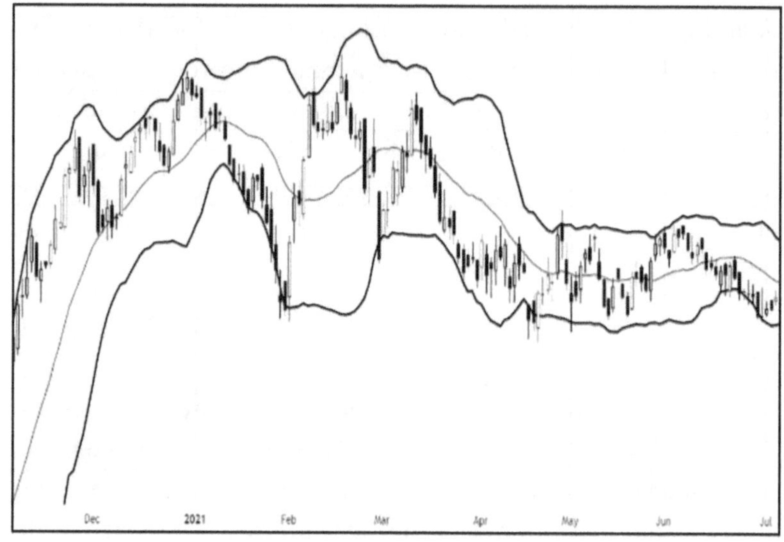

Chart 8.8

Supertrend:

A Supertrend is a trend following indicator just like the moving averages. It is an indicator that gives an accurate reading about an ongoing trend. The default values used while constructing a super indicator are 10 for average true range or trading period and three for its multiplier. However, these settings can be changed.

"The average true range (ATR) plays an important role in 'Supertrend' as the indicator uses ATR to calculate its value. The ATR indicator signals the degree of price volatility.

For a long position, you can put stop loss right at the white indicator line. For a short position, you can put it at the black indicator line.

Using Supertrend along with a stop loss is the perfect way for earning the best wealth in trading.

Supertrend works best in trending markets, both uptrends and downtrends. The buy-sell signal can easily be identified. A buy signal is generated when the Supertrend closes below the price and the colour changes to white. On the other hand, a sell signal is made when the Supertrend closes above the price and the colour of Supertrend turns black. Have a look at the following chart (Chart 8.9) of BAJAJ FINANCE, showing buy and sell signals on 15 minutes timeframe.

Chart 8.9

Just like all the other indicators, the Supertrend can also fail some time. It can generate false signal in a range bound market. However, when compared to other indicators, the Supertrend indicator gives less false signal.

Volume Indicator:

This indicator simply tells us how many trades were executed on any given day. For every buy and sell, the volume adds up to 1. For example, if on a particular day, 1,000 contracts were bought and sold in a particular security then the volume is 1,000 and not 2,000.

High volumes are indicated by large bars whereas, low volumes are indicated by short bars. If a pattern or signal is confirmed and there are high volumes, it is the best situation for entering into the trade.

Look at the chart 8.10 which shows volumes in INFOSYS on daily timeframe.

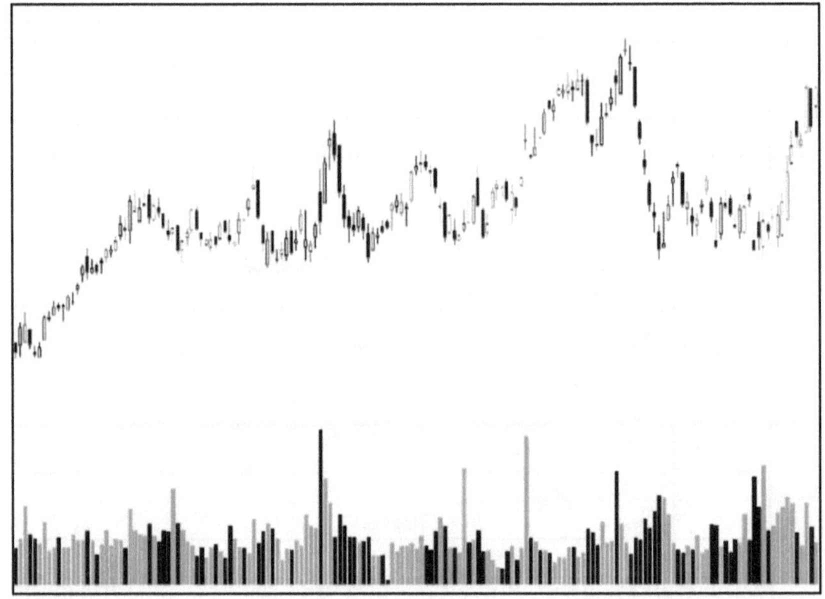

Chart 8.10

(Volume Indicator proves very useful when it comes to confirming breakouts)

As discussed earlier, the indicators should be used to confirm the entry or exit points. One should never rely solely on the indicators for entering the trade. True reversal signals are rare and can be difficult to separate from false alarms. There can be situations when even the golden or death crossovers can fail, the RSI might be showing bullish divergence but the price will still continue to fall down, etc. Hence, one thing is clear, the indicators should be used in combination with some other indicators or chart patterns to increase the chances of a profitable trade. For using any indicator, we only need to open the chart of a particular stock that we want to track. Trader can set the timeframe as per his trading style. For intraday the timeframe of 5min or 15 min is preferable.

With this information I would like conclude this chapter with a little advice.

Try to understand these indicators by applying them across few stocks of your choice. The more you practice these techniques and study the chart patterns, the easier it will become for you to identify them in future.

9. WHAT IS MEANT BY FUTURES AND OPTIONS

In this chapter we will be learning about various concepts related to FUTURES and OPTIONS trading.

(A) Options trading:

Options are a form of DERIVATIVES and they derive their value from the value of an underlying asset.

Options were launched with the purpose of reducing risk for the asset owner. When someone holds assets, there is always a risk that the asset may lose value in the marketplace. With the help of options this risk can be transferred to other people who are willing to accept it in exchange for a payment.

The simplest example to understand this concept is the premium paid by us for health insurance. We get health insurance to transfer the financial risk to the insurance company in case anything happens to us. The company is ready to take the risk in exchange of monthly premium. But what is the reason that the company is willing to take the risk of you facing huge medical bills?

The company takes the risk upon calculating the probabilities. The insurance company is betting that the probability of them paying out huge sums of money is very low. On the other hand, we are willing to pay the monthly premium amount because we want to be assured that if something happens to us, our medical expenses are taken care of.

This same thing happens in options market. The option buyers hope to participate in the potential gains in the underlying asset.

Others are sellers of options as they believe that the potential gains that the buyers are expecting will never appear.

In options trading, the trader can make profits when the underlying asset moves up, down or even sideways. The number options that can be traded are not limited like the stocks issued by the individual companies.

Options are contract to Buy or Sell a specific number of shares of the underlying asset at a specific price and at a specific date in future. The number of shares, which is also known as lot size, controlled by one option contract is different for different assets in India. You can get the information about the lot size of different assets on the official website of National Stock Exchange. The lot size for Nifty Options is 50 and for Bank Nifty it is 25 as of now (April, 2022).

Types of Option Contracts:

There are two kinds of exercise style which are normally used in derivatives market, European and American. European options are those options which cannot be exercised before the expiration date. This means that the option buyers can exercise their right only after expiration. On the other hand, American options are those which allow the flexibility of exercising the options at any point of time till expiry.

In India, all equity and index options are currently exercised as European options. One way to quickly identify whether an option is a European or American style is to look at the nomenclature of the option contract. If there is CE in the contract name then it is a **CALL European style** option. Similarly, CA in the contract name means **CALL American style**. On the other hand, PE in the contract name indicates a **PUT European style** option and PA means **PUT American style** option.

A trader buys a CALL option when his view on the underlying asset is bullish, expecting the price of underlying asset to go up, and buys a PUT option when he/she is of the view that the price of the underlying asset will fall, i.e., bearish view.

For every buyer in the options market, there is a seller. When a trader sells a Call option his view is bearish on the security in which he has traded indicating that he expects the price of underlying asset to fall. A Put seller is of bullish view, expecting the underlying asset's price to rise.

Rights of the option BUYERS and SELLERS:

The call buyers have the right to purchase the underlying asset at a specific price and at a specific date in the future, but do not have any obligation to do so. Likewise, the put buyers have the right to sell shares of the underlying asset at a specific price and at a specific date in the future without any obligation.

The opposite is true for the Sellers. The seller of the call option is obligated to sell the shares of the underlying assets in case the buyer of call option exercises his right to buy them. On the other hand, the seller of put option is also obligated to buy shares in case the buyer of put option exercises his right to sell.

Most of the option contracts are not exercised. The main goal of option traders is to gain profit from the difference between the selling price and the purchase price of the option.

If an option expires unexercised the buyers/holders of the options contract no longer have the rights available in the contract.

Option Premium:

Option buyers get the right to buy or sell the shares of underlying asset after paying a certain amount to the option sellers. This amount paid by the buyers is known as **Option Premium**. While the buyers account is debited by the premium paid, the sellers account is credited by the premium received.

Option premium changes as the price of the underlying asset changes.

Strike Price and Expiration Date:

The **strike price** is the specific price at which the options trader can buy or sell the underlying asset or shares at a future date. The spot price is the price at which the underlying asset is trading currently in the market.

All the stocks that can be traded in options will have options for various strike prices. Option buyers and sellers are not entitled for any dividends when the underlying company issues them.

The specific date in the future till which point the trader can buy or sell options of the underlying asset is called the **Expiration Date**. In Indian market, the expiration date for equity options is always the last Thursday of each month, whereas, for Index options, the expiration is every week on Thursday. If there is a trading holiday on Thursday, then the expiration will be on the previous trading day.

Stock options have a maximum of 3-month trading cycle, the near month (one), the next month (two) and the far month (three). A new contract is introduced on the trading day following the expiry of the near month contract. The new contract will be introduced for a duration of three months. This way, at any point in time, there will be 3 contracts available for trading in the market i.e., one near month, one mid-month and one far month duration respectively.

ITM, ATM and OTM Options:

For a call option, when the strike price is lower than the price of underlying asset's price it is known as **In-the-Money** (ITM) option. The put options are said to be ITM option if the strike price is higher than the underlying asset's price.

A call and put options are said to be **At-the-Money** (ATM) option if the strike price is very close to the underlying asset's price.

A call option is said to be **Out-of-the-Money** (OTM) option if the strike price is higher than the price of underlying asset. On the other hand, a put option is said to be OTM if the strike price is lower than the underlying asset's price.

All OTM options expire worthless at expiration. But do you know what is an extrinsic or intrinsic value? And why do the OTM options expire worthless? To answer that, let us move ahead.

Intrinsic and Extrinsic Value:

The premiums of every option are made up of two components, intrinsic and extrinsic value.

Intrinsic value is the difference between an option's strike price and the underlying asset's price, whereas, the **Extrinsic value** is the difference between the market price of an option (its premium) and its intrinsic value.

OTM options do not have any intrinsic value. For ITM call options, the intrinsic value is calculated by subtracting strike price from the asset price. For example, Nifty is trading at 16,200, then the intrinsic value for 16,100 Call option is 100 (Asset Price i.e., 16,200 − Strike price i.e., 16,100).

For ITM Put options, the intrinsic value is calculated as the strike price *minus* asset price. For Example, if Nifty is trading at 16,200, then the intrinsic value for 16,300 Put option is 100 (Strike Price i.e., 16,300 − Asset price i.e., 16,200).

The extrinsic value or ITM options, whether call or put, is calculated by subtracting the intrinsic value from option premium. Once you find the intrinsic value, whatever option premium remains is the extrinsic value. For example, consider, Nifty closes at 16,300 at expiry and the premium for 16,200 Call option Rs.128.50. Hence, extrinsic value in this situation is, 28.50

(Option Premium i.e., 128.50 – Intrinsic value i.e., 100 = Extrinsic Value i.e., 28.50)

As the intrinsic value for OTM options is zero, they do not have any extrinsic value. Hence, extrinsic value of OTM options goes to zero at expiration which results in them expiring worthless.

Settlement of option contracts:

Options are settled either physically or in cash. Index options are settled in cash whereas, stock option contracts are settled physically.

In physical settlement, the trade completes with the transfer of the shares of underlying security from the seller to the buyer, i.e., when the seller of Call option delivers the shares of underlying security to the call option buyer or when the seller of put option gets the shares delivered by the put option buyer.

Cash-settled options are trades that pay out in cash at expiration, rather than delivering the underlying asset or security. When settlement is made in cash, the amount of payment usually is the difference between the option strike price and the current value of the security at the exercise date.

Cash-settled contracts are relatively simple to deliver because they require only the transfer of money. An actual physical delivery has additional costs attached to it. Cash-settled contracts are one of the main reasons for the entry of speculators and, consequently, bring more liquidity to derivatives markets.

Risk Involved for the traders:

Before entering into anything, we should always know about the risk involved in it. This becomes even more important when the money gets involved.

The risk for option buyers, whether call or put options, is only the amount which is paid as a premium. The potential gains that the call and put option buyers can experience is unlimited. For example, Trader A, buys BANKNIFTY 35,000 CE option at the premium of Rs. 175. Hence, the premium paid is Rs.4,375. This is the maximum amount which the trader can lose.

The same goes for the Put option buyers. If trader B buys BANKNIFTY 35,000 PE option at Rs.125, he/she can only lose the premium amount paid of Rs.3,125.

Hence, the buyers are safe as they have inbuilt stop loss.

On the other hand, an option seller is not so fortunate. We will see this with the help of an example. Consider, a trader who sold the 500 Put option of SBI stock and received the premium of Rs.6,000. Now imagine what if the stock price falls to Rs.0? In this case let us see the total loss that the seller may suffer. (The lot size for SBI while writing this book is 1,500)

$$\textbf{Seller's loss} = [(0 - 500) \times 1{,}500] - 6{,}000 = \textbf{Rs.7{,}56{,}000}$$

You can see that this is a huge loss in comparison to the profit that the trade would've generated. This proves that the risk for put sellers is high till the underlying security reaches 0.

The case for Call sellers is even worse. Consider the seller of the 500 Call option and receives the premium of Rs.4,500. What if something happens and the price of SBI rises to say Rs.5,000 per share?

In this case, the loss of the trader would have been unimaginable.

Seller's loss = [(500 – 5,000) x 1,500] – 4,500 = Rs.67,54,500

Though the probability of this happening is very low, it shows the risk involved in selling the options. So, **NEVER** take this risk lightly. The maximum amount that a seller, whether put or call, can gain is the initial premium received.

The table 9.1 will summarize the characteristics of the options.

Trader's action	Nature of Option	Profits potential	Losses potential
Buy Call	Bullish	Unlimited	Limited
Sell Call	Bearish	Limited	Unlimited
Buy Put	Bearish	Unlimited (till the underlying security reaches 0)	Limited
Sell Put	Bullish	Limited	Huge (till the underlying security reaches 0)

Table 9.1

Example:

Consider there are two parties, Mr. X (buyer) and Mr. Y (seller), entering into a contract. Mr. X wants to buy a land which Mr. Y is selling as he thinks that the price of the land will increase due to some government project whereas, Mr. Y is selling the land because he thinks that the price of the land will decrease due to a news he heard about the cancellation of the project. The seller wants to sell the land in say Rs.10 lakhs. The buyer enters the contract of buying the land after 1 month by paying the token amount of Rs. 1 lakh (Premium). The seller agrees to enter the contract by receiving the token amount.

If the price of land increases to Rs.12 lakhs (Spot Price) after one month then buyer can exercise his right to buy the land at the price of Rs.10 lakhs. The seller will be obligated to sell the land at that price. In this situation the buyer will have a profit of: 12 lakhs (current price of land) – 10 lakhs (pre-determined price) – 1 lakh (token amount) = Rs.1 lakh.

On the other hand, if the price of land decreases to Rs.9 lakhs after one month then buyer won't exercise his right to buy the land waiving off the token amount paid to the seller. In this situation the seller gets to keep the token amount of Rs.1 lakh as the contract expired and was not exercised.

This is exactly what happens in options contract. The 10 lakh is the strike price whereas 1 lakh is option premium. Expiration is after 1 month. 12 lakhs and 9 lakhs are the spot price on expiration.

Leverage and Hedging:

Leverage and hedging are the few concepts you should know before you start trading in options.

Leverage is a double-edged sword. We can either make a lot of money or lose a lot. As we know, in options a single lot controls a lot of shares. The lot size for different stock is different. The concept can be explained in a better way with the help of the following example.

Consider, the stock of State Bank of India (SBIN) is trading at Rs.500 per share on 10th April, 2022. The lot size for SBIN is 1,500 at this time meaning that a single contract controls 1,500 shares of SBIN. You think that the stock price of SBIN will rise due to a positive news which will be announced. Assume you have Rs.8,00,000 with you for investment. You can do two things in this case, either you can buy the stock itself or buy an ITM call option.

If you prefer to buy 1,500 shares of SBIN, it will cost you 1,500 x Rs.500 = Rs. 7,50,000. But if you buy one contract of 450 strike call option, you will need 1,500 x 50 (assuming the option premium to be Rs.50) = Rs.75,000. So, if you prefer to invest the entire amount available then you can buy 10 contracts for a total of Rs.7,50,000, i.e., 75,000 x 10 = Rs.7,50,000. It means you are currently controlling total of 15,000 shares of State Bank of India with the same capital as required for buying 1,500 shares. The trader may choose to buy any number of contracts be it 1, 5 or 10.

This is the power of leverage we get in options. One thing you should keep in mind is the risk gets lower if the trader prefers to buy just one contract. But instead of buying 1 option contract if the trader buys 10 contracts the risk involved would be same as in the case of buying the stock i.e., buying 1,500 shares. Many beginners wipe out their entire capital as they focus only on leverage ignoring the risk.

So, as a trader you should be careful while using leverage.

Hedging in simple language means using options to protect against losses in your existing portfolio. For example, if you own long positions, then the hedging will protect the fall in prices of those positions. On the other hand, if you have short positions then the hedge will protect you against the rising prices of those assets.

If the trader hedges 100% of his/her portfolio, he will have no losses, but no profits either. Different traders may choose different percentages of their portfolio to hedge. Some may prefer to hedge 80% of their portfolio if they are comfortable with 20% fall in their investments.

For example, there are two traders, Mr. A and Mr. B, holding 1,000 shares of IRCTC at an average price of Rs.700.

Mr. A buys, ITM put option with strike price of Rs.740 with a premium of Rs.43.

Mr. B buys OTM put option with strike price of Rs.680 by paying a premium of Rs.4.75.

Situation 1: The price falls to Rs.650.

In this case, both the traders would suffer a loss of **Rs.50,000**, i.e., (700 – 650) x 1,000, without a put protection.

As Mr. A have hedged his portfolio with a 740 put position. His holdings will show a loss of Rs.50,000. However, the put option with the strike price of 740 will be worth: (740 – 650) x 1,000 = Rs. 90,000. He paid the premium of Rs. 43 for buying the put options. Therefore, his total profit prom the put option is: 90,000 – (43 x 1,000) = Rs.47,000.

Due to the put hedge, the overall position of the Mr. A, will have **a loss of Rs.3,000 instead of Rs.50,000.**

On the other hand, Mr. B have hedged his portfolio with a 680 put option. The worth of this put option will be: (680 – 650) x 1,000 = Rs. 30,000. He also paid a premium of Rs.4.75 to buy this put option. Therefore, his total profit from put option will be: 30,000 – (4.75 x 1,000) = Rs.25,250.

As the result of the put hedge the overall position of Mr. B, will have a **loss of Rs.24,750 instead of Rs.50,000.**

Situation 2: The price reaches back to Rs.700 at expiration.

At this point, both the traders will be at **breakeven**, meaning no profit no loss, without a put protection. But when traders have hedged their position, the situation will be different.

For Mr. A, the 740 put option will be worth: (740 – 700) x 1,000 = Rs. 40,000. The premium paid by Mr. A was Rs.43,000. Therefore, total loss in the hedge will be: (40,000 – 43,000) = Rs.3,000.

As the holding is at breakeven, the overall position of Mr. A, including the put option will have a **loss of Rs.3,000.**

For Mr. B, the 680 put option will be worthless at expiration. Therefore, the loss in the put option will be the amount of Rs.4,750 which was paid as premium.

As a result, the overall position of Mr. B, with put option will have a **loss of Rs.4,750.**

Situation 3: The price rises to Rs.780 at expiration.

In this situation, the portfolio of Mr. A and Mr. B will be in a profit of Rs. 80,000 without hedging.

With hedged position, Mr. A will have a gain of Rs.80,000 in the portfolio but the put option with 740 strike will be worthless.

Therefore, the total premium paid by Mr. A to buy the put option will be the loss in the hedged position, i.e., Rs.43,000.

Hence, the overall position of Mr. A with hedging will show **profits of Rs.37,000**, i.e., 80,000 − 43,000.

On the other hand, for Mr. B, the put option with strike price of 680 will expire worthless as it also expired OTM. This will result in the put option making a total loss equal to the premium paid, i.e., Rs.4,750.

Thus, for Mr. B the overall position with the hedge will be showing **profits of Rs.75,250**, i.e., 80,000 − 4,750

We can see that the trader who buys the ITM put option for hedging is sacrificing some upside profits to keep the losses small whereas the one who buys an OTM put option for hedging will have big loss if the stock falls heavily and can gain more money than Mr. A on the upside move.

Conclusion:

Mr. B gains more profit than Mr. A on the upside.

When the stock stays near the original price, both the traders will make a very small loss equal to premium amount.

Mr. A will be in a better position if the stock falls heavily whereas, Mr. B will make more loss.

With these examples, I hope you have understood the topic of options trading. Next on the list we have futures trading.

(B) Futures:

Futures are similar to the options. A futures contract is also a contract between a buyer and a seller in which, the buyer agrees to buy a specific number of shares or an index from the seller, at a pre-mentioned time in the future for a pre-determined price. Futures are traded on the exchange just like we trade stocks and options. Here, the buyer and the seller of a futures contract are obligated to fulfil the agreement at the end of the expiry.

For example, if someone wants to buy a futures contract of ITC for the expiry of May (one contract control 3,200 shares of ITC when writing this book). This means that they make a futures contract that they will buy 3,200 shares of ITC from the agreed price as of May expiration whatever the market price at that time. The seller also agrees to sell those 3,200 shares of ITC at the agreed price.

Now both the buyer and seller are obligated to buy or sell these shares unless they trade with other buyers or sellers and exit the position before expiry of the contract.

The futures contract can be traded easily. If the traders' views change then they can just transfer the contract to someone else and then get out of the agreement, at any time. In the futures contract, the terms of the contract are constructed according to an official standard and they cannot be negotiated.

The futures contracts are time-bound as they end on the expiry date and are mostly cash-settled, removing the tension of moving the physical asset.

The trading cycle for futures is same as that of options the only difference is there is no weekly expiry in futures contract as in index options. Hence, we can trade the near month, the next month and the far month expiry. A new contract is introduced on the trading day following the expiry of the near month contract just like in options.

Traders can also buy futures of commodity, index funds, foreign currency exchanges, etc. You can visit the NSE website to see the details of any stocks or index futures contract.

Do note, Investors have a risk of losing more than the initial margin amount as futures use the leverage.

(Margin amount is the part of the total value of the futures contract that the buyers or sellers are required to deposit. This deposit is required as per the regulations set out by exchange, and must be deposited before a futures contract is bought or sold. Margin money is essentially a guarantee that the trader will honour the contract. After entering into the futures contract, the margin amount is blocked in the demat account).

Hedging can also be done using futures contract as in case of options. When someone have long position in a particular stock and want to protect any losses due to fall in price, he/she can sell (short) the future contract. On the other hand, one who has a short position in a stock he/she can buy the future contract to counter any rise in the prices of the stock.

Open Interest:

Open interest (OI), is a number that tells us how many futures or option contracts are currently outstanding in the market. For every buyer there is a seller. When the buyer and seller enter into one contract the OI is said to be 1. This means that the open positions in the market is one. The transfer of contracts does not increase the OI. OI increases only when traders enter into new contracts.

OI data includes the open position till they are closed and volumes change on a daily basis.

Traders use the volume and OI data in association with price action to make a view about the market.

123

Having said that, we will move on to the next chapter where we will study about the impact of Options Greeks on the option premium.

10. OPTION GREEKS

The Greeks are essential tools in risk management that can help options-traders make informed decisions about what and when to trade. They help to look at how different factors such as price changes, interest rate changes, volatility, and time affect the price of an option contract. In short, the Greeks refer to a set of calculations you can use to measure different factors that might affect the price of an options contract. With that information, you can make more informed decisions about which options to trade, and when to trade them.

The Greeks change as the underlying asset changes, sometimes they do this rapidly if expiry is close.

These are the Greeks we will learn about:

- Delta.

- Gamma.

- Theta.

- Vega.

- Rho.

Delta:

Delta is the Greek which measures the sensitivity of the option to the movement of the underlying asset. It indicates how much the option premium will change if the underlying asset change by 1 point, i.e., 1 Rupee in Indian market.

Deep ITM Calls tend to have deltas approaching 1, whereas, far OTM Calls tend to have deltas approaching 0.

Similarly, deep ITM Puts will have delta close to 1 and far OTM Puts will have delta closer to 0

An option with a strike price very close to the underlying asset price, i.e., ATM option, will have delta close to 0.5

In a call option, if the price of an underlying asset rises, the delta also rises whereas, if the price falls, then the delta value also falls. On the other hand, in case of a put option the delta rises if the price of an asset falls and vice versa.

In simple words, Delta measures the probability of the option being ITM at expiration. Therefore, it is logical to say that an At the Money option should have a delta close to 0.5 as there is 50% chance that the underlying asset will be above current price and 50% chance that it will be below the current price at the time of expiry.

Let us consider an example to understand this concept better. If a stock is at Rs.200, then the current month's call option with strike price around Rs.600 will have a Delta close to 0. This simply means that the probability of the price reaching Rs.600 before the expiry date of the option is almost zero. For the same stock, the call option with strike price of Rs.250 will have Delta near to 0.5, i.e., there is 50% chance that the price will reach Rs.250 before or at the expiry. Similarly, the call option with strike price around Rs.100 will have delta near to 1 as the probability of stock price staying above Rs.100 is almost 100%

In case of the Put Options, the case is inverse, i.e., strike price of Rs.600 will have delta close to 1, strike price of Rs.250 will have delta near 0.5 and strike price of Rs.100 will have delta near 0.

Delta is positive when one buys a call option or sells put option. In both the cases the view is that the price of underlying asset will rise. When the trader buys a put option or sells call option, he thinks that the price will fall. In these cases, the delta is negative measuring from -1 to 0, depending on the option (ITM, ATM or OTM).

Call Buyers (Long Calls) will have Positive Delta:

Traders buy call options when they think that the underlying asset's price will rise.

When we buy call options (bullish view), any increase in the price of underlying will cause the option premium to rise by the amount indicated by Delta, resulting into profits for traders. On the other hand, any decrease in the price of underlying asset will reduce the option premium by the amount indicated by Delta, resulting into losses for traders.

Put Buyers (Long Puts) will have Negative delta:

Traders buy put options if they think that the price of underlying asset will fall.

When we buy put options (bearish view), any increase in the price of underlying will cause the option premium to fall by the amount indicated by Delta, resulting into losses for traders. On the other hand, any decrease in the price of underlying asset will increase the option premium by the amount indicated by Delta, resulting into profits for traders.

Call Sellers (Short Calls) will have Negative Delta:

Call options are sold if the price of underlying asset will fall according to the trader.

When call options are sold (bearish view), any increase in the price of underlying will cause the option premium to rise by the amount indicated by Delta, resulting into losses for traders as the difference will have to be paid by us at the time of squaring off the position. On the other hand, any decrease in the price of underlying asset will reduce the option premium by the amount indicated by Delta, resulting into profits for traders as we get to keep the premium.

Put Sellers (Short Puts) will have Positive Delta:

Put options are sold if the trader is of the view that the price of underlying asset will rise.

When put options are sold (bullish view), any increase in the price of underlying will cause the option premium to decrease by the amount indicated by Delta, resulting into profits for traders as we will get the premium amount, whereas, any decrease in the price of underlying asset will increase the option premium by the amount indicated by Delta, resulting into losses for traders as we will have to pay the difference when we square off the position.

The profits or losses in the cases mentioned above shows the effect of Delta on the position. However, we know that Delta changes for every point move. But how is it decided by how much the delta will change for every point move in the underlying asset? To know the answer, we will move on to the next Greek, Gamma.

Gamma:

Basically, Gamma is a Delta generator. It indicates how much the Delta of your position will change when the underlying asset's price moves by 1 point. It tells us how much more Delta will be added or subtracted from our existing Delta with a one-point change in the asset.

The Gamma for long positions is positive and for short positions it is negative. If you own 1 ATM call option with delta of 0.5, and the Gamma of the position is 0.1, then if the underlying increases by 1 point, your call position's new Delta will be around 0.6. The new increased Delta is due to the positive Gamma. Your profits will increase on your long position (while buying call or put options) as the Delta increases.

Now consider, what would have happened if you were short on the same call with delta on -0.5. Delta would still have increased, but this time it would be -0.6. In this case you will lose money as you have sold the call option, which is gaining in value. So, the Gamma is said to be negative for your short positions (while selling call or put options).

As the position draws closer to expiration, Gamma can have a great effect on Delta for options near the money. Gamma is highest for ATM options and tends to be near 0 for OTM and deep ITM options.

As the price of underlying asset moves, the ATM option will have to change most. Hence, the gamma is highest for ATM options. If the option is far OTM, then any movement in the underlying asset's price need not have any significant effect on those options. The Gamma is near 0 in initial stage and therefore doesn't change the delta which is also near 0. However, as the price rises and the options goes from far OTM to slightly OTM and then ATM, the gamma also rises which increases the delta value resulting in the options premium to rise.

The logic for deep ITM option is same as it is for far OTM options. The delta is near 1, Gamma is near 0, which means that the price movement of the asset is not sufficient to change the probability of this option from being ITM. However, the situation might change if the price of asset continues to move towards this option's strike price.

Theta:

Theta indicates how much the option premium will change as the time passes. As discussed in the previous chapter, the extrinsic value of options goes to 0 as the expiration of the option approaches. Theta is the measure of how much the extrinsic value will decay each day as the options approach expiration. Theta is highest for ATM options. Deep ITM and far OTM options have Theta closer to 0.

Theta is said to be friend of option sellers because the option premium received by the seller will decay everyday generating more profits in the position (if the other greeks remain constant). On the other hand, it can be considered as an enemy for option buyers as the premium paid for buying option, whether call or put, will reduce each day by the amount of Theta, which will result in losses (other greeks being constant).

Theta decays rapidly near the expiry. Most of the novice traders make the mistake of buying OTM option near expiry and lose money even if the asset moves into the direction of their expectation. They wonder what went wrong. This happens due to the effect of Theta decay also known as time decay. If the underlying asset doesn't move far enough and fast enough before expiry, the long trade will lose money because of THETA! I can say this because this has happened to me. The 1st time I traded was without having the knowledge about the greeks. And that's when I understood how important it is to know about greeks.

Let's take an example. Suppose, a trader buys BANKNIFTY 36,000 call option on Wednesday (while Bank nifty is trading at

35,600), with premium amount of Rs. 65, Delta is 0.15, Theta is - 30, thinking that Bank Nifty will move above 36,000 before expiry which is on Thursday. In this case the probability of this strike price being ITM by expiration is only 15% which is very low. What will happen if Bank nifty moves only to 35980 by expiration? The trader will lose the entire amount of premium paid (1 lot x Rs. 65 = Rs. 1625).

This is common scenario where trader buys OTM options due to their "cheapness" compared to ITM options. They ignore the fact that the probability of OTM option making money is far less than ITM option. However, OTM option can also prove profitable depending on different market scenarios.

Vega:

This Greek is related to Volatility in the underlying asset. If the stock price moves a lot, whether up or down, then it is said to be very volatile.

Vega is a Greek that measures the option's sensitivity to implied volatility (Implied volatility is a number which indicates what the market is suggesting about the volatility). It measures the amount of increase or decrease in an option premium based on 1% change in implied volatility of the underlying asset. If a stock has large price fluctuations, the implied volatility in the options will be higher and vice versa.

When buying options (Long position), whether calls or puts, the Vega is always positive. When volatility rises, long positions benefit from it.

On the other hand, when selling options (Short position), either calls or puts, Vega is always negative. When volatility rises these short positions start making losses.

Consider, you have bought NIFTY 17,000 Call option (Vega is positive for long positions). For every 1% rise or fall in volatility, the trader will theoretically make or lose money due to Vega. If the market goes up, then you will make money because of Delta, but lose money due to Vega, as implied volatility usually drops when markets go up. For Put option, the scenario is different. If you have bought NIFTY 17,000, Put option, and the market falls, then your position will not only make profits because of Delta but also due to Vega. This happens because implied volatility rises as the markets go down, and long positions have positive Vega. Hence, the position will gain profits.

Vega is highest for ATM options and lowest for far OTM options. Beginners often buy options without paying attention to the effect of recent volatility. Then as the volatility gets crushed, the options purchased by them becomes cheaper without any major movement in the underlying asset. So as a trader, one should always give Vega the respect it deserves.

Rho:

Rho represents the rate of change between an option's value and a 1% change in the interest rate and is expressed as the amount of money an option will lose or gain with a 1% change in interest rates. This measures sensitivity to the interest rate. For example, assume a call option has a rho of 0.15 and a price of Rs.185. If interest rates rise by 1%, the value of the call option would increase to Rs.200, all else being equal. The opposite is true for put options. Rho is highest for at-the-money options.

However, Rho is considered to be the least important of all option Greeks.

I would recommend you to read this chapter again and again so that you get your concepts related to the option Greeks cleared, which in turn will help you in great way in your trading journey.

11. TRADING IN STOCK MARKET

As discussed in the previous chapters, trading in stock market involves investing, swing-trading, day trading, trading in derivatives like futures and options. These can be classified into intraday, positional, swing, medium or long-term trading.

Traders complete the entire transaction in a single day in intraday trading, whereas, in positional trading, they carry forward their positions which gives them more time than intraday traders for trading.

The short-term trading refers to trading which is carried out within few days or few weeks. The medium-term trading being for 1 to 3 years and long-term trading having time period of more than 3 years.

Trading is often considered as "GAMBLING". There is always a story in almost every Indian family that someone who was trading in Stock Market has lost everything and had to even sell his/her house or properties.

To be very blunt, if the situation arrived where one had to sell their house, then they surely were gambling. According to me, anything that you do without knowledge and without any control is Gambling. I recall something I once heard somewhere which I am going to mention here, ***"Agar market me paisa leke aaoge toh gyan leke jaoge aur agar gyan leke aaoge toh paisa leke jaoge"*** (If you enter the market with only money, then you will take away knowledge with you. But, if you enter the markets with knowledge, then you take money with you). This is the harsh reality of the market.

The market can give you everything if you are disciplined enough and stick to your trading plan/trading setup, but if you are unable to control your greed and fear, fail to trade as per the plan and do not follow the rules, then the market will show no mercy to you and will wipe out your capital.

Now, how does the situation arrive where one has to sell properties, assets or house?

Anyone doesn't arrive at this stage directly (or that's what I Believe). This is a result of consecutive mistakes made by the trader over a period of time. Let us take an example to understand this. Consider, a trader, Mr.X, who trades in options has a capital of Rs. 15,00,000. Instead of learning about risk management, money management, psychology, position sizing, trading plan, etc. he decides to deploy the entire capital into options. He makes a profit of Rs. 2,00,000 on his first trade. He again makes profit of Rs. 3,00,000 on the next trade. Now he has a capital of Rs.20,00,000, he enters a position with all of his capital. Then his stop loss is triggered (Loss=Rs.1,50,000), but he refuses to exit and holds the position hoping for something good to happen. The loss increases to Rs.3,00,000. He now decides to exit when the loss reduces to Rs.1,50,000. You can see that the trader is holding the loss-making trade. The position shows a loss of Rs.5,00,000. Now he is praying that the loss should be reduced and is still holding the position. By the end of the day, he had to exit the position with a total loss of Rs.7,50,000.

This happens few more times, he earns something then losses big. After few weeks, he has left with a capital of Rs. 1 lakh. Now he wants to recover his capital. He assures himself that once he recovers his capital, he will leave trading. He has learnt nothing about "Cutting the losses short and holding onto the winning trades".

He again starts trading, makes profit in few trades and losses in some. But as he has no control over his greed and fear, he loses the remaining 1 lakh too.

After blowing up his entire account (Losing entire capital), he tries to find some other strategies as he thinks that, the strategy he was using might not be good. He watches few videos on the internet trying to find a strategy with 100% accuracy, the Holy Grail.

He takes a loan of Rs. 30 lakhs and enters the market again with a different strategy. The same thing happens again. He takes small profits from markets and gives big losses.

At the end, he is left with debt of Rs. 30 lakhs, a lot of mental stress and keeps on cursing the market and calling it as gambling. And there is nothing wrong about his view towards markets. What he did was truly gambling.

Psychology plays a main role in trading. It is so important that I have dedicated a separate chapter only to discuss the psychology involved in trading.

Now the question which still remains is, how to protect our capital from being wiped out? What are the dos and don'ts while trading? How to become a better trader?

In this chapter we will try to get answers to such questions with the help of few important points.

Importance of Rule-based Trading:

We have seen in the example at the start of this chapter how the capital of Mr.X was wiped out as he didn't follow the rules. But what does the rule-based trading means?

As the name suggests, there are some rules that a trader must follow in order to be profitable trader. It means that the trader should enter the trade only if there is entry signal as per his setup which may include trendline breakout, support or resistance breakout, chart pattern formed and breakout given by the underlying asset, etc.

The trader should always enter with a predefined stop loss and target. Stop loss can be placed just below or above the levels where the breakout happened, whether upward or downward breakout.

Risk to Reward Ratio (RRR) of at least 1:2 should be followed by the trader. This means that if the trader takes a risk of Rs.5,000 he should have a reward of Rs.10,000. This has to be done for simple reasons. For example, consider, you have entered a trade where you made a loss of Rs.5,000 exiting the position when the SL hits. In the next trade you earn a profit of Rs.10,000, following the RRR of 1:2. You close the day with a profit of Rs.5,000. Hence, it is always recommended to trade with RRR of 1:2 or at least 1:1.5.

One should exit the position when the target is achieved or trail the SL if one wishes to capture bigger movement. To trail a SL basically means placing the SL at a level where you will still be in profits if the trend reverses. When the trailing SL hits, the position should be exited. Traders trails the SL in order to capture big movement after their target is achieved.

You should only trade till you hit 3 stop losses in a day. If you hit 3 SL in a day just close your trading devices and stop trading for that day. We will understand this with the help of an example. Suppose, I entered the 1st trade and had to exit as SL (Rs. 5,000) was triggered. The 2nd trade also resulted in a loss of Rs. 5,000 as SL was triggered again. Now I entered the 3rd trade, if in this trade I achieve target i.e., Rs.10,000 profit then I will be in a no profit no loss situation and therefore, can continue trading on that day. But if my SL gets triggered again in the 3rd trade too, then I will have a total loss of Rs.15,000 and even if I made profit in my 4th trade, I will still be at loss of Rs.5,000 but making a loss in the 4th trade will increase the losses. Therefore, we should only accept 3 stop losses per day.

If there is no entry according to the setup for the entire day, one should not enter any trade. It is not necessary to trade daily. You should enter the trade only if the price is at the levels marked by you. Discipline matters the most in trading.

Always remember one thing, "Market is Supreme". If you learn how to cut your losses then there is nothing that can stop you and the market will reward you handsomely. But if you fail to follow the rules, then market will definitely take everything from you.

Importance of Right Position Sizing:

One of the most important things to remember while trading is to trade with right position size. You should not increase the position size as soon as the profits increase. It should be increased slowly. The reason is simple. If you increase the position size as soon as you start making profits then you might gain big profits, but due to the bigger size of the position the losses also are big. This will impact your psychology. Let us understand this with the help of an example. Suppose, you are trading in Nifty options with 5 lots (50 x 5 lots = 250), you are making good returns. After few days of earning consistently by following rule-based trading you decide to increase the position size to 20 lots. At this point you are used to see the figures related to 5 lots. You could easily handle 20 points loss in 5 lots as it was only Rs. 5,000 and it didn't have a big impact on you. But with an increased position size, i.e., 20 lots (50 x 20 lots = 1,000), even a fluctuation of 3 to 4 points will show the loss of 3 to 4 thousand. When your SL of let's say, 20 points, gets triggered it will show a loss of Rs. 20,000 which you won't be able to digest quickly.

Hence, position sizing is also an important aspect of trading that a trader should understand.

Avoid Big Losses:

A trader can be in 4 situations while trading which can be small profits, small losses, big profits and big losses. The only thing a trader has to focus is to avoid the big losses. The SL helps us to avoid the big losses. The small profits will take care of small losses and big profits will keep you going.

Risk Management:

Risk management helps to cut the losses short and help the traders to save their capital from getting wiped out. A trader can lose all the profits made by him in just two or three bad trades without proper risk management. Risk management means having a predefined Stop loss, target and keeping the Risk to Reward ratio of at least 1:2.

You should diversify your investments across various industry sectors. If you put all your money in one stock or one instrument, you are risking it all and might even end up with big loss. One can also hedge their positions as discussed earlier to protect the losses.

There is a famous phrase among the traders, "Plan the trade and trade the plan". It means traders should always plan their trades before they execute them and trade according to the plan.

On the other hand, Money management is nothing but a proper balance between risk and reward. The position sizing is also a part of money management.

Avoid Overtrading/Revenge Trading:

Overtrading or Revenge trading, as the name suggests, means trading excessively. This happens when a trader has already incurred losses on a particular day. He takes different positions to recover the losses, which leads to more losses most of the times.

Sometimes the trader trades even after earning big profits in order to earn more and gets Greedy. If he incurs loss then he takes another trade to make the profits amount same as before. This is known as overtrading. One should know when to stop.

Also, remember the charges you have to pay on each trade executed. If you have overtraded and are in net loss at the day end, then you will also have to pay the charges which only adds up to the negative flow of money from your trading account.

The bottom line is, *avoid overtrading and respect the market.*

Maintain a Trading Journal:

A trading journal can be either a book or an excel sheet where you keep the records of your trading activity. It should contain the date, script name in which you have traded, buy/sell, entry price, exit price, time, quantity, etc.

Maintaining the journal helps a lot as you can see how you have grown as a trader over the years and learn from your past mistakes.

You can make your own format for recording your trading activities in the journal. Look at the following format for example.

Date	Time	Script	Buy/Sell	Entry Price	Quantity	Exit Price	Profit/Loss	Rules Followed?	Remarks

The column named remarks can be used to mention your emotions during the trade or whatever you think as important to mention. Whereas, in the rules followed column you should write yes or no.

Take Responsibility for your losses:

The trader should take responsibility for the losses he suffers rather than blaming the market and bad luck. However, he should not live in the past thinking about the losses he incurred previously. He should just trust the process and trade as per the rules.

Never take LOAN for trading:

Most of the time people make the mistake of taking loan after they have lost their capital while trading expecting to recover the amount. But when they fail to do so, they lose the loan amount too. Now, they also have to repay the loan amount. This affects the trader mentally and increases the stress.

In this situation, the trader should first of all repay the loan amount. You should arrange the capital by working for some more time and have sufficient amount kept aside so that your day-to-day expenses are easily taken care off, then start again with proper rules.

If you follow these above-mentioned rules and act accordingly then you can definitely grow as a trader.

Let us now discuss few pros and cons of trading.

Pros of trading:

1. Trading has unlimited potential.

2. It can give you multifold returns on your investment.

3. You can have control over your life.

4. It can help you to achieve financial freedom.

5. You can complete your dreams which might require more money.

6. You can take holidays when you want.

7. If you know how to trade, then you can even complete your trades within couple of hours.

Cons of trading:

1. Trading can take everything from you.

2. You could end up wiping out all of your savings.

3. There is high risk in trading.

4. You can also make losses that you couldn't handle.

Hence, one thing is clear, you should never start trading only because you know someone who earns in lakhs every day and thinking that you will to the same. Those who earns in lakhs have different capital and different risk appetite. They have spent more time in the market than you. It might have taken them years to reach the position where they stand today. So, if you think that stock market is some get rich quick scheme then you should stay away from the market.

We are now left with only few small topics to discuss. So, without wasting much time, let us get going.

12. TRADING AS A CAREER

Trading can be exciting and even profitable if you are able to stay focused, do due diligence, and keep emotions aside. Stock market is a field where money is made from money. If you want to make a career in stock market, you can either be a stockbroker, Investment Advisor, Financial Advisor, Financial Analyst, Equity Analyst, etc. or you could be a trader. We will discuss about being a trader.

One can choose to be a trader and can make fortune in it if the rules are followed by the trader. But there are certain things that one should consider before entering into trading as a fulltime career. Making day trading your full-time job is not easy, and it likely will not happen immediately after you start. However, you are always the one in total control over your investments and, ultimately, profit. Being a day trader means you set your own hours, govern your own actions and only do what you truly believe in. One of the main reasons people are attracted to investing as a career is that they gain total personal liberty over their day.

But if you are thinking about leaving studies to start fulltime trading then you should drop that thought right now. The first thing you should do is to complete your education so that you have a security. Once you have completed your education you can get a job to arrange capital for trading, then start trading side by side with low capital. I would suggest a new trader to start with Rs.10,000. While trading during this time, the SL and target rule should be strictly followed, note down your mistakes and learn from them.

When you have spent enough time in the market, have arranged enough amount (excluding the capital for trading), that can take care of your expenses for at least 4 to 6 months and won't affect your family financially, then you can start trading fulltime if you feel so. Initially everyone will tell you to think about your decision again, but if you can follow proper trading rules and can keep your emotions aside then ask them for some time and prove yourself by becoming a profitable trader.

If somehow, you end up blowing up your capital but are determined to become a trader then stay away from the markets for some time, find out what went wrong for you, learn from the mistakes and arrange the capital again by doing jobs. The amount saved for daily expenses for 4-6 months should not be used for trading because if you use that amount and lose that too then it will have a huge impact on you financially as well as mentally.

And for those who are still studying and want to trade, first focus on your education, try to arrange capital for trading by working part time. *"Do not BORROW or take LOAN to trade"*. When capital is arranged by your part time jobs, you can trade alongside your studies. Learn and grow with every trade you take.

Market is the greatest teacher, if you follow the trading rules then there is nothing that can stop you. If you want to choose trading as a career, you should generate income sources that can take care of your expenses.

Keeping it short and simple in this chapter let us now get to the conclusion this chapter.

Conclusion:

- Trading can be chosen as a career but there is a process to become a trader that should be followed.

- Leaving education for trading is not an option.

- Generate income sources that can take care of other expenses so that you can trade.

- Discipline in trading is must.

13. PSYCHOLOGY INVOLVED IN TRADING

Psychology plays the main role in trading. Trading is 90% psychology and 10% skills according to me. Even if you possess all kinds of skills and also are a great technical analyst, but if you cannot control your emotions and are not psychologically prepared then you cannot survive in the stock market. Trading psychology represents various aspects of an individual's character and behaviours that influence their trading actions. Traders should not make decision based on extreme emotions such as anger, fear, anxiety, greed, excitement, etc. Emotions are one of the key reasons why individuals make irrational choices.

Greed and fear are the two main psychological factors that should be controlled while trading.

GREED can be thought of as an excessive desire for wealth, it results into affecting the decision making and rationality. Greed may lead to a trader or investor to stay in profitable trades longer than it is advisable, in hope for extra profits which might result into loss.

FEAR causes traders to exit the position earlier to avoid large losses and taking small profits. Fear can cause traders to act irrationally in their rush to exit the position.

For example, if you have achieved your target but didn't exit the position as you are expecting for more or wait for the losses to reduce or turn into profits, letting the greed take over your decision-making capability then it will result into small profit or big loss. On the other hand, if you let fear enter in your mind while trading and couldn't exit the position after your stop loss gets triggered or exit the position before the target is achieved then it will ultimately add to your losses or result into small profits.

Therefore, it is most important to trade as per the rules and strictly follow the plan. You should trade like a robot, if target is achieved, exit the trade. If SL is triggered, exit the trade.

There may be situations when your target will be achieved after hitting your stop loss. But what if you didn't exit the position and it results into a bigger loss?

If you have a right strategy and trade as per the plan, then even if you have a success rate 60% then it will have a great impact. Let us see this with an example.

Suppose, a trader keeps a stop loss Rs.5,000 and target of Rs.10,000. He executes 10 trades out of which he suffers losses in 4 trades and is profitable in 6 trades. Thus, his total loss is Rs.20,000 (i.e., Rs.5000 x 4) and total profit amounts to Rs.60,000 (i.e., Rs.10,000 x 6). Hence, the net position is Rs.40,000 surplus. People don't pay attention to this. They want big profits and want to make money quickly. But they fail to understand the importance of consistent profit making, consistency is the key.

The main point of discussion is, you should first prepare your psychology by trading with a low capital. If you cannot handle Rs.10,000 then you also cannot handle Rs.1,00,000 or more. Immediate success cannot be handled as the mindset is not ready for it.

For example, if I trade in 100 qty then I can handle the profit and losses as my psychology is developed for this quantity. But if I start trading in quantity of 10,000 then every point fluctuation will show me either profit or loss of Rs.10,000. As my psychology is not developed for such big quantity, I will either make an impulsive move or do something against the trading plan which can put me in big trouble. Therefore, we should increase our position size slowly as discussed earlier.

Avoid trading when in a bad mood, feeling sleepy, travelling, family function, etc.

Write your thoughts during trading.

"Hope and Regret" are the other things that play crucial rule in trading.

HOPE may cause a trader to hold onto a loss-making trade hoping for it to turn into a profitable one.

Whereas, ***REGRET*** may cause a trader to enter a trade after missing out on it as the stock moved too fast. This is not a sign of a disciplined trader. Such trades will result in losses as the price might start falling from peak highs. Consider this as trying to catch the missed train.

Individuals also tend to become overconfident about their analysis, knowledge or skills, even if they are not up to the mark. They should avoid decision making in such overconfidence.

You could also practice paper trading using demo account. There are many apps which provide a demo account for traders to practice trading. However, it will not develop your psychology as the money involved is not real. This is also the reason you should start trading with low capital in order to build your psychology.

I hope you understood the importance of psychology in trading.

14. BUSTING THE MYTHS

This chapter is a little addition which I decided to include in this book as I reached to this point. In this chapter we will have a look at few myths related to the Stock Market one by one.

1. Stock Market is Like Gambling:

The comparison of the STOCK MARKET to GAMBLING is just like Indian parents comparing their kids with "Sharmaji ka Ladka/Ladki" (Pun intended).

Gambling refers to winning or losing by chance whereas, stock market investment depends on many factors including the market history, the present economic conditions and information about the company you want to invest in as discussed earlier. Hence, the Stock Market is nothing like Gambling if you know what you are doing and have sufficient knowledge about the stock market.

2. You Can Only Make Money if you have large Capital:

This myth has been developed from the belief that to make profits, one must have a huge capital to survive the losses which the trader might incur while trading which isn't true. The share market offers opportunities for traders with variety of risk appetites and capital.

You can invest in shares for as low as Rs. 10-50. The important task to do is to find the right company through proper research and to develop a strategy to minimize your losses from the beginning.

3. Only Experts can trade and invest in Stock Market:

Anyone can participate in the stock market and make profits and create wealth. Investing in the share market requires proper understanding of the market and identifying the right shares. But, this process of learning is continuous and develops over time. The share market is open to anyone with a keen interest in the market.

4. Higher Risk means Higher Returns in the Stock Market:

Some of the high-risk investments in the stock market indeed prove profitable to traders. However, it doesn't mean that investments with high risk will generate high returns all of the time. In fact, the probability of losing in high-risk investments is same as that of winning.

5. Investing or Trading based on the tips provided by others through social media:

Many people invest and trade based on the tips they get from their friend, family or some other sources claiming 90% or even 100% accuracy. However, the best way to make profits from the stock market is by spending time in the market and doing your own research, understanding the market and the current trends and then invest as per the strategies formulated.

6. Owning more stocks means having more diversified portfolio:

Having a diversified portfolio doesn't mean you have to own more stocks. Consider an example, if you carry more apples than what you can carry then you cannot handle all the apples and some of them will fall. In simple words, it will become hard to track all the stocks. So, one should diversify his/her portfolio in few stocks of different industries rather than investing in 2-3 companies of each industry.

Epilogue

Stock market investments require sufficient research and preparation. Once an investor/trader is able to do this, they can utilize the wealth creation potential of the market.

If you have reached till this point then I would like you to appreciate yourself for taking time to learn something new and finishing what you started. This is all the information that I could provide in this book. I hope this book proves helpful in your journey as a trader. Even though this book has cleared most of the concepts related to the stock market, there is so much for everyone to learn other than this.

I would also like to thank you for choosing this book as a stock market guide for you. I also hope that now, if someone mentions to you that Stock Market is Gambling, you can explain them how it is not. You don't need to argue with anyone as they are not wrong, they are just not well-informed.

I wish you all the success and growth in life and hope this book proves helpful in your journey as a trader. Read this book again if you didn't understand something and practice whatever you have learned in this book.

If you learnt something from this book and feel that someone should read this then recommend this book to them and help them.

I know that you will definitely become a trader if you do the right things in a right way at the right time.

Till then, Happy Trading!!